2020

2020

Making Sense of Madness

by Tony Milne

Published by Handmaid Books

This edition published in 2021

Set in Times New Roman
All designs by Tony Milne

ISBN-13: 979 872 5792911
This edition printed by KDP

tonymilne.net

Preface

We saw in 2020 the COVID panic that trashed the global economy, the confrontations between Brexiteers and Remainers that resulted in Britain's withdrawal from Europe, and the end of Donald Trump's divisive policies and their replacement by equally divisive ones. Hardly in the background, activists attacked racism, police brutality, pollution, and the burning of fossil fuels. The forces of law and order oppressed racial and religious minorities, and attacked civil rights activists, while governments used their protection to fund and encourage greater consumption, pollution and violence. Meanwhile, western nations ignored the real problems of stagnant populations, massive debt, crippling taxation, and unaccrued financial obligations that will not be met even by the next generation of tax-payers.

Criticising incompetent leaders, demagogues and the naïve voters, readers, listeners and watchers fails to address why humans behave this way. Claims for human intelligence, stupidity, cupidity, or incompetence fail on close examination.

Fortunately there is an explanation for such behaviour. This explanation is simple, clear, and covers both the growth of human civilisation and its collapse. It describes the process whereby individual human actions multiply their effects by involving the masses. It dismisses the role of intelligence or stupidity, malice or benevolence, as mere colour and disguise, which disappear when seen from a suitable point of view in good light.

I set out with this book to describe the world we can all see today. It explains how to interpret the seemingly inexplicable behaviours of the key individuals, the leaders and the followers; those who tell others what to do, and those who do it, or refuse to do it. I explain why governments end up implementing useless and costly programmes instead of effective and efficient ones. I will even explain why members of government implement actions that reduce the short-term tax take, even though they know that it will likely cost them (and many others) their jobs to make up for it. I also explain our role as tax-payer, voter and citizen in supporting them in their ineffective and costly behaviour.

This explanation does not seek to blame; on the contrary, we are all responsible through our unconscious though observable, interactive behaviour.

It may not give much hope for our future as a community but, knowing how humanity works, it may enable us as individuals to understand, prepare for and perhaps change our own future. It will certainly help us to prevent our own behaviour exacerbating the problems we face.

Tony Milne
In lockdown
December 2020

2020

Making Sense of Madness

Contents

Introduction

The year 2020 may go down in western history books as the year in which it all started to go wrong. There were certainly ominous signs before then but, by 2020, it was clear that governments in western democracies had no idea what they were doing and, if anything, their interventions only made things worse. Yet, the system that produced them still kept the support of the voters, and the forces of law and order protected them, to the extent of killing, wounding or attacking those few who resisted.

The search for explanations of other epochal moments often refer to intelligence. It is considered as being important, if not the most important factor, in the development of human society. It permits, so the hypothesis goes, the creation of political, legal, religious and social structures, which support urban populations, nation states, trade and travel. [1] However, although this hypothesis supports an explanation for the rise of great empires, it does not explain their subsequent collapse, and every empire eventually collapses.

Periods of imperial decline could have been reversed by the application of intelligence, in the same way that it had served to create the empire in the first place. Intelligence would always have been able to deal with whatever problems they faced, had the citizens applied it. That they did not indicates that intelligence

---

[1] A popular recent success based on this idea is Yuval Noah Harari's *Sapiens*. [190]

is not applicable in periods of decline, and suggests that it is no more used in periods of growth.

Other explanations for human success include the selfish gene, altruism in its various forms, tit-for-tat cooperation, morality, and culture, all personal traits which humans can claim to possess to some degree, thereby sharing in the glory of the species' success in building great civilisations. However, they fail to explain why the same people, doing the same things, manage to destroy them. The selfish gene, in particular, fails to explain its often disastrous behaviour in the extinction of its species, a fate common to many of its possessors, not just humans.

Explanations for imperial collapse range from social to environmental, passing through moral, military, technological, or religious. The common factor among these excuses is blame. It is always someone or something's fault, lead poisoning, climate change, foreign invasion or corruption. However, the ubiquity of imperial collapse makes it unlikely that environmental or foreign influences merely a proximate cause. Rome was invaded by Gauls and Carthaginians, and became stronger as a result, Venice was afflicted by the Black Death and bounced back, Europe grew to global dominance during the Little Ice Age, a period which saw considerable nutritional stress throughout the region. A strong nation can survive such influences, which are likely to afflict its weaker neighbours more heavily and for longer.

The duality of human character is often ascribed to explain the rise and fall of nations, especially those of a religious character, starting with the *Bible*. The assertion that humans are good, intelligent, moral, cooperative when things are going well, and evil, stupid, corrupt and selfish when things are going badly, may be true of observations made of individuals, but does help to describe the fate of the great societies of history or to predict the fate of the present ones. The behaviour of a crowd or a herd has little to do with individual impulses. [2] Descriptions of human behaviour based on later outcomes fail to explain behaviour in real time, and don't help to predict outcomes at all. It is easy to say after the fact that the Roman empire declined due to Christianity, or that the Spaniards conquered the Aztec empire because they were cannibals, but these are not descriptions of behaviour, but ascriptions of abstract nouns to groups of individuals.

If these are not the reasons for human success and failure, then it is worth seeking the real reason to understand how Europe came to dominate the world and now seems incapable of managing its own affairs. To do this, it is necessary to look back in human evolutionary history to a time when humans didn't build civilisations, and investigate what has changed since then.

All the available evidence suggests that until quite recently, humans behaved in ways that were common to many mammals, most primates and all apes. The males lived in tight communities of close kin who cooperated to hunt, defend their territory and their females, the women might migrate from their birth group to other groups, and different groups would avoid or attack each other. All wild mammals possess this fight/flight/freeze instinct to ensure competition for

---

[2] [25]

resources and mates. It effectively prevents co-operation outside the kin group, the small number of family members with whom an individual has grown up.

Less than seventy-five thousand years ago, human beings underwent a significant behavioural change. The new behaviour that some adopted was the most important in making human beings the social animals we recognise today.

The change involved losing the natural mammalian instinct of fight/flight/freeze on encountering a strange adult male of the same species. Humans replaced this instinct with a simple interaction that immediately permits co-operation between unknown adult males. More importantly, it permits co-operation between large groups of adult males.

Whatever is the largest kin group possible for any primate, the combination of two or multiple groups in any competitive activity would result in victory. The evolution of this trait permitted a weaker and even a less intelligent ape to dominate any other primate, and any other animal.

This change, however, had an immediate cost, not least the psychological cost, but it also permitted a delayed profit. It guaranteed mating opportunities, if slightly delayed, without having to fight for them. It permitted young adult males to remain in the group for longer, or to separate and form new groups. It allowed groups to travel and still find other groups with whom to co-operate. Above all, it permitted small kin groups to co-operate as much bigger groups, to defend territory against other groups or predators, to hunt, to migrate.

The change was responsible for an immediate success. Co-operating groups of humans could dominate or exterminate those who did not co-operate, through superior numbers. However, the real benefit arose when these multiple groups came to an agreement about the sharing of resources. Once an agreement was in place, and there was confidence in that agreement, individuals could start to invest. They invested their time and energy and preparing ground, fertilising it planting crops and irrigating them, protecting the field from herbivores; they invested in livestock, protecting them from carnivores. They invested in irrigation canals and granaries. They invested in brine boilers, in the pottery to speed up the process, and more canals to bring the brine to fires. They invested in ever more complex tools. The agreement with other groups permitted trade in raw materials and finished goods. Trade encouraged greater communication, especially of knowledge. Co-operation provides the basis for all the technology and civilisation that is necessary to support a human population of billions.

Co-operation, however, is not the behaviour, but the outcome. Co-operation has a positive sense, when it involves large numbers coming together to build a cathedral or a legal system.

This change in human behaviour led to the increase in human population, far beyond that of any other large mammal. This increase applied pressure to other predators, which saw a decrease in their population, and an extinction of many of their species.

The behaviour of modern humans permitted the co-operation of large numbers to build cathedrals, cities and civilisations. However, the same behaviour, innate, instinctive, genetic, continues regardless of environment, of circumstances. Humans behave in that way while living in the desert and in the Arctic tundra, in the wealth of a harvest season and the dearth of winter, in the glorious growth of an empire and in the imperial decline. Humans co-operate to destroy a building or an empire. Humans even co-operate in their own destruction, the pollution of their environment, the total extraction of their natural resources, the suicidal declaration of war on a more powerful enemy, the overpopulation of their territory,

Europeans behaved in the same way during the five hundred years that they dominated the world commercially, technologically and culturally, and during 2020 when they became the laughing stock of the rest of the world, destroying their economies, cuffing their oft-recited liberties, and breaking up their civilisation.

This behaviour, seen through the news of 2020, is the subject of this book.

2020

The last five years have seen a political world in turmoil. The current imperial hegemon, the United States of America, suffered from the conflict engendered during the Trump presidency and its determination to *make America great again*. The last imperial hegemon, the United Kingdom, struggled to implement Brexit and its stated goal to have *no foreigner telling us what to do*. The immediate effect of the policies implemented by their elected leaders was to make the British and American stated objectives less likely. Both sets of policies were divisive, encouraging national and international confrontation, separatism and demagoguery. Both were supported by barely 50% of the electorate, with the other 50% proposing an equally ruinous, but diametrically-opposed, alternative.

In 2020, most of the world was struck by a new strain of coronavirus, a virus which attacks the upper respiratory tract and can lead to lower respiratory tract infections, serious illness, pneumonia, multiple organ failure and death. COVID-19, as it became known, rapidly expanded to become a pandemic.

The World Health Organisation and most governments have well-prepared plans for dealing with pandemics and epidemics. These generally focus on the early identification, notification, isolation and treatment of those infected. There is also a general promotion of healthy lifestyles. The best protection against respiratory tract infections caused by viruses like

COVID-19 is clean, fresh air and sunshine. Access to these resources is usually free and tax-free.

Instead of following the scientific and agreed preparations for dealing with COVID-19, many governments around the world banned exercise, locked people in their homes and forced them to wear masks outside. Stuck in the putrid dryness of air-conditioned and double-glazed homes, breathing behind a mask, and with only the occasional trip to the shops for a hand rub with alcoholic gel, the population rapidly succumbed to the virus. A million people died in the northern hemisphere spring season. The global economy suffered from these government measures, collapsing ten percent in some countries, with long-term impacts on unemployment, travel and trade. Worse still, they will affect governments' ability to raise funds through taxation and will increase borrowing to pay for the additional social and health care. Inevitable tax increases to pay off the panic can only further depress the economy, leading to additional costs and more tax increases. Countries with stable or stagnant populations will struggle to pay off these debts.

At first sight, British government behaviour in dealing with Brexit or American government behaviour in general appears driven by wilfulness, incompetence, ignorance, political expediency, opportunism, or even by conspiracy. However, many governments confronted by COVID are behaving in the same irrational way. In most countries around the world similar measures are implemented, with complete disregard for science, professional medical practice, the official advice of WHO, or even the common sense of people with their own experience. [3] The opposition parties actively support and comply with government measures, in spite of ever increasing evidence of their unpopularity and ineffectiveness.

There are suggestions that some government and health ministry officials are using the Brexit, Trump or the COVID crisis for personal Machiavellian reasons, in other words, they are intelligent, or at least cunning. However, the failure to achieve any material success in their political campaigns, their policy reversals, their stuttering postures and obvious confusion are clear evidence that this is not the case. Intelligence or cunning are not the hallmarks of political animals, although a thick skin certainly helps along with a dose of shamelessness.

The ubiquity of government action to deal with COVID, the popular reaction, and their counterparts throughout recorded history, indicate that such behaviours stem from something much more innate than intelligent or unintelligent decision making, whether evil or benevolent in intent. Rather, the inescapable conclusion is that this behaviour is driven genetically. The coronavirus is merely the trigger for these innate, genetic, behaviours, which are programmed and prepared for such an opportunity. They are the symptoms of circumstances, and predictable in their appearance.

---

[3] It should be clarified that WHO and other health organisations have official publications. Individuals working for WHO or government health ministries may appear on television or in the media and make pronouncements, but these should not be confused with recommendations based on scientific procedures resulting from investigation and research.

However, it is unlikely that genes causing early death, economic downturn, or physical injury would survive worldwide in our DNA, unless they also lead to demographic growth. Genes appear through human behaviour. Therefore, in the search for an explanation, it is necessary to recognise in advance that only such behaviours that are able first, to create the world powers of Britain and the USA, and a global population vulnerable to coronavirus, will satisfy as an explanation for their destruction.

This theory requires cognitive dissonance to accept and even more to understand. However, the behaviour should be readily observable. It cannot be a superficial and abstract concept, such as *building a strong economy*, or *providing health care facilities* for the population. Rather, the observation of specific interactions between individual human beings should highlight those that can both improve the economy and demography and, perhaps later, destroy the infrastructure and civilisation that they have created. The important points are that the behaviour must be the same at both stages, regardless of the surrounding economic and social situation. That behaviour must implicate everyone, without giving them a choice to avoid it. Any choice will simply allow a genetic return to the mammal origin of fight/flight/freeze, in which the fighter will kill the co-operator and end his participation in the gene pool.

Identifying the behaviour and its genetic origins is not easy, but there are several clues. Government measures implemented to control the pandemic make it clear that taxation is a principal factor in government decisions, whether it is conscious or unconscious.

Measures selected for enforcement, such as lockdowns and mask wearing, put the onus of compliance on the citizen, the tax-payer. More effective measures, such as identification, isolation and treatment of infected individuals, would become the responsibility of tax-collectors, the civil servants and the political heads of medicine and government. In many countries, including almost all so-called western democracies, these behaviours are unenforced, leaving nobody in government accountable.

One common theme among the leaders of the western world is their contravention of the very rules that they impose on the general population, whether it is to spruce up their hair-do, visit a girlfriend, play golf, or simply do their job in a manner that is most comfortable for them. Those with the greatest expertise and experience in control of the disease, the government ministers responsible and their healthcare advisers, considered the measures they introduced to control it unimportant.

Heads of government showed high rates of infection. [4] Their co-morbidities, especially of obesity,

---

[4] Donald Trump, Boris Johnson and Emmanuel Macron are the most famous and relevant COVID cases, all caught as a result of ignoring calls for social distancing. Trump refused to wear a mask, Johnson participated in physical cabinet meetings and Macron kissed visiting dignitaries. Other leaders include Prince Albert of Monaco, Nuno Gomes Nabiam of Guinea-Bissau, Mikhail Mishustin of Russia, Nikol Pashinyan of Armenia, Juan Orlando Hernandéz of Honduras, Jair Bolsonaro of Brazil, Jeanine Áñez of Bolivia, Alexander Lukashenko of Belarus, Alejandro Giammattei of Guatemala, Andrzej Duda of Poland, Abdelmadjid Tebboune of Algeria, the alliterative Boyko Borissov of Bulgaria, and the late Ambrose Dlamini of Eswatini. During 2020, 15 heads

usually euphemised to diabetes, and respiratory problems caused by smoking and urban pollution, should have labelled them as vulnerable and led to their obligatory isolation. If there is one group of workers whose work is not essential, it is that of government. They produce nothing, transport nothing, care for nothing and consume vast quantities. Instead of self-isolating, they infected each other with gay abandon, and spread the disease throughout the world. They continued to work and play, while banning both for the rest of the population.

One explanation might be that humans, and politicians are ultimately human, are intelligent creatures, and that something has gone wrong with the application of that intelligence. This faulty application may be due to faulty data, wilfulness, the stupidity of certain individuals, propaganda from some evil conspiracy, the deliberate attempt by a foreign power to destabilise the economy, or merely an accident in time which will eventually sort itself out.

Another explanation may be that governments or their members, as seen by their detractors, are evil. Equally, governments blame criminals, terrorists, greedy bankers, lazy trade unionists, adolescents, drug traffickers and foreigners, rather than the declining global economy.

---

of state or government caught COVID, 4% of their peer group, compared to 2% of the global population. Only 1 died, due to a co-morbidity, although Pierre Nkurunziza of Burundi may have died of COVID. Internet lists of leaders, politicians and members of royal families show that these people have a total disregard for the rules of social distancing, essential travel only, and the avoidance of physical touch.

There is little evidence for any claim that others are to blame as individuals, and no evidence at all for the dualism inherent in any assignation of evil motivations. Greek philosophers debunked ethical dualism two thousand five hundred years ago. Psychologists now call this *attribution error*. This is a tendency to make excuses for ourselves (and, by extension, people we agree with or love, our in-group) that we won't make for others (the out-group). This prejudice against foreigners prevents co-operation and improvements that could be garnered from it. There is no place in any scientific, academic or intellectual work for such concepts as good and evil to explain human behaviour. [5]

More common as explanations of perceived government failure are the ideas of incompetence and conspiracy, which seem to contradict each other. Anyone who has ever tried getting half a dozen people to agree on a course of action, even an erstwhile

---

[5] However, in *Tax Man*, the author makes the case that, if the point of view is taken as that of the entire human species, and that, if the objective is agreed to ensure the greatest possible instantaneous population, then the imprisonment, mutilation and murder of tax-payers and potential tax-payers are behaviours detrimental to the achievement of the objective. The best behaviour to achieve this objective is for tax-collectors to take about 10% and the best behaviour for tax-payers is to acquiesce; the result should be the best economic and demographic growth possible under the prevailing geographic, climatic and geopolitical circumstances. Taking the point of view of an individual, it is always possible to identify desirable courses of action that favour an individual, as opposed to the entire human species. However, individual success usually comes at a price, and tax-collectors ultimately suffer more than the tax-payers they oppress.

pleasurable activity like going for a meal or a drink, knows that conspiracies are totally unrealistic ways to run entire countries full of millions of wilful people.

Incompetence is perfectly acceptable as an excuse for the failure of modern organisations, of which national governments are the largest, richest and most powerful. Incompetence in government is especially noticeable when it involves someone else's government. In modern democracies, with either no political party majority or a very similar support for each of two major parties, then half or more of a nation's population may consider their government incompetent.

If incompetence is a reasonable suggestion for our current woes, and the explanation for our previous disasters, then intelligence fits neatly into the role as the generator of human success, its demographic growth and expansion into every ecological niche, the creation of art, architecture, music, literature, political and diplomatic systems, medical, engineering and informatics technologies, as well as crazy flights to the moon and to the bottom of the oceans.

There is no doubt that intelligence plays a part in human civilisation, however that is defined, but equally there are too many examples of incompetence to pretend that intelligence is the major factor. Given a choice between two courses of action, any government minister can choose the better one half the time. Therefore that selection is no longer the result of intelligence but of a simple and random process.

More complex decision making shows up the real failure of intelligence as a major demographic driver. Civilisations, nation states, international corporations and NGOs operate under many constraints, need to satisfy innumerable stakeholders, and have constantly changing terms of reference. Decisions made in such circumstances depend far more on politics than on intelligence, or perhaps it would be correct to say that the role of intelligence is directed towards gaining the political support of those stakeholders, rather than choosing the course of action that will result in the greatest economic and demographic results.

Politicking is not a skill unique to human beings. Mammals do it to some extent, all primates do it and the apes are experts at it. Perhaps humans are better at it than chimpanzees and gorillas, but the behaviour is not unique, so it is unlikely that the enormous difference in population between the other great apes and *Homo sapiens* comes solely from their slightly greater ability to manage the search for support in the community.

The final issue that needs resolution is the fact that every human civilisation, whether from ancient past or recent modern history, has collapsed or suffered conquest. Ur of the Chaldees, Troy of Priam, Athens, Rome, Tikal of the Maya, Constantinople, Tenochtitlán, Cusco of the Incas, Delhi, Beijing, Berlin, Madrid, Amsterdam, Tehran, Babylon, Cairo and Paris have resounded to the heels of the enemy jackboots or the haunted weeping of the ghosts of their history. [6]

Whatever are the factors that lead to great development, huge cities, trade empires and industrial developments, the same factors must operate somehow to lead the same people (genetically) living in the same

---

[6] London and Washington suffered conquest, but only before they became the capitals of great empires. Lisbon has survived the loss of its empire without invasion.

geography, surrounded by the same neighbours, to decline. Equally, human beings run governments in the most successful economies and demographies, in China and in the United States, as well as in the abject failures, Rwanda, Afghanistan, Cuba and North Korea. The same human species which ran China in the 1950s, when the behaviour of its people caused the greatest loss of life ever, is running it today, when it has shown the greatest sustained economic growth of any nation ever. The same human species that ran the United States to global superstardom in the 1950s is running it today, when it has multiple trillion dollar debt and whose civil conflict plays out nightly on television like the reality show of some dysfunctional state.

To say that human behaviour was intelligent in the United States of the 1950s and in the China of the 21st Century, and that it was incompetent in China in the 1950s and in the United States today does little to improve understanding of humanity. It also ignores the disastrous 1950s policies of American intervention in Central America, Korea and Vietnam or the Cold War generally, and Chinese behaviour towards its own citizens, especially ethnic minorities and its successful billionaires, today.

Neither intelligence nor incompetence can play a major role in human demographic development, either in its growth or in its decline. Clearly both, together with accident or luck, will affect matters for a year or two, but empires that grow over a hundred years and then collapse in a hundred cannot be affected by the intelligent decision, nor by the incompetence, of one or two people.

Intelligence is a magnet for those ascribing our world domination, but there is just insufficient evidence to support this noble but misleading idea. Equally, incompetence is a popular insult but rarely survives close contact with those directly involved in decision making. Fortunately, it is possible to use intelligence both to refute the idea and to discover the truth, the real reason for the up-and-down nature of world geopolitics, the frustrations felt by both governors and electors, that doesn't involve blaming the others, inventing satanic motivations, or creating myths and heroes, whose statues history will topple.

The behaviour of governments, health ministries, non-governmental or supra-national organisations, scientists, doctors and the media can be explained, without recourse to easily debunked theories, dualism, or grandiose and abstract notions. There is also a logical explanation for the often rapid escalation of aggression, violence, imprisonment, mutilation and death that accompanies such behaviour. Such an explanation can even make sense of the inconsistencies in the behaviour of governments.

The only reliable basis for interpretation of human behaviour is the physical expression of that behaviour which observers can record, compare and analyse as an actor and an act. In human society, the behaviour that can explain social development usually involves a third party, the victim.

The analysis of specific behaviour, as opposed to the categorisation of behaviours, is more common in the learning environment, especially the objective-driven competency models used in business and adult-learning. The need to assess current skill levels, define training goals in behavioural performance terms, and implement training programmes to bridge the gap, creates a structure in which outcomes, the training goals, and behaviours, can be analysed, and the training behaviours measured for effectiveness. This provides an economic model of behavioural efficiency at achieving specific goals that is easy to transfer to an evolutionary investigation.

In the long-term evolution of the human species, the only interesting fact is population and, in particular, its growth. Subsidiary factors, like geographic spread, ecological niche occupation, interaction with other species, are all interesting in themselves and as a subsidiary to the main point, but are irrelevant. If there is no population growth in the core group and territory, then there will be little selective pressure to move and occupy other geographic or ecological niches, nor with the relations with other species change over time to much effect.

This work takes as its basis, therefore, the evolutionary objective of population growth. This choice makes no ethical or moral judgement on growth or population, nor on its effect on other species. The purpose is merely to identify that behaviour or those behaviours which lead to significant population growth. Human population is vastly greater than that of any other large wild mammal, and only comparable in numbers to sheep, and in biomass to cattle. This population was achieved only in the last few thousand years, before which, with all the advantages of bipedalism, great intelligence, technology and culture, our population was no greater than that of any other large predator, like the hyena, dogs, cats and bears.

It is likely, therefore, that the specific human behaviour responsible for the massive growth in the species' population evolved only recently, and has little to do with the morphology or intelligence which evolved hundreds of thousands of years ago.

Homo sapiens

It is conceivable that the first conscious act of the first modern human, the first member of the species *Homo sapiens,* was to say to himself, after a first and particularly impressive accomplishment, "Boy, am I smart, or what ?!" Humans are not uniquely self-conscious, but there is no evidence that other apes, whales, elephants or dogs think of themselves as intelligent. Self-definition is a unique character of human beings, and the definition chosen by that first human, and repeated endlessly to today's blockbuster book, is that of intelligent man, *Homo sapiens*.

History of Self-Congratulation

What prehistoric humans thought of themselves, how they referred to themselves, and how they saw themselves as different from other species is impossible to know for sure. From historic times, however, those responsible for documenting life recognised a significant difference between themselves and others, and between themselves and the rest of Nature in particular.

The earliest works of writing in Western culture, such as the *Epic of Gilgamesh* or the *Bible*, put humanity at the centre of the story, usually with a *deus ex machina* who provides some good advice from time to time. The early stories show the value of cunning. It is low intelligence, perhaps, but intelligence nevertheless. The noteworthy behaviours highlighted are mainly illegal now, but the lack of real punishment gives a good indication that humanity had already adopted the concept of ethical dualism to frame its actions, to justify its crimes.

The combination of absolute obedience to authority, together with lying, cheating, stealing and murdering his fellow humans, pervades the doctrine of the Old Testament, as does the disparagement of logic or book-learning.

Adam and Eve are punished for seeking knowledge from the Tree of Life, and the punishment is to have to work for a living; the corollary is that those who don't work with their hands, like priests and government ministers, must have some god-given dispensation and should be treated with respect. Cain is rewarded for murdering his brother by having a large family, including the wealthy copper- and iron-smiths and the popular musicians. His family history is confused, but he could be the great-great-great-grandfather of Noah. Noah was intelligent enough to obey blindly every instruction from his god. By such behaviour he averted the flood that wiped out curious, questioning, doubting humanity. Noah's family and descendants have profited ever since.

One of Noah's descendants was Abraham. Abraham was similarly obedient to his god, prepared to sacrifice his own son on the whim of a nameless, invisible spirit. His own descendants included Isaac and Jacob. Jacob used his cunning to gain his elder brother's inheritance, and went on to dupe his uncle by using genetic engineering to steal away the greater part of their common flock.

Later biblical heroes include Joseph, who founded the tax state in Egypt. He took 10% of all the food production and then gave it back during a drought, but only to those who first surrendered their land. The great intelligence of Joshua brought them to the Promised Land, where they had their greatest moment under the kings. David was not just a brave warrior-lad but also a poet and musician, while Solomon, a byword for intelligence, was adulated by his contemporaries and had a thousand concubines.

Jews produced their own philosophers who argued that intelligence was not Greek cleverness but the fear of Yahweh. Faith reigns supreme, and empirical, scientific knowledge was somehow banal, terrestrial, even prosaic. [7]

The Bible formed the documentary basis for a new religion, or at least for a religion for a new group of people, that of Christianity. Its earliest hero was an iconoclast, using Greek logic and critical reading of the Scriptures to embarrass the priests and administrators. They scourged and crucified him. The new religion built up around his myth of submission to authority and the pervasiveness of spirituality, and ignored his iconoclasm and anti-authoritarianism. For its adherents, the Church insisted on obedience to dogma that was characterised by *Santa Sophia*, the holy wisdom. This dictated that the supreme intelligence was to believe in God and obey his representatives on Earth. This ultimate insult to intelligence was both popular and successful. For five hundred years, the Church stifled intellectual thought.

---

[7] [23]

The administration of the christian Church took a much more practical approach than what was recommended for the faithful. Based around the classical Roman education of its priests and monks, Christianity formed the backbone of European expansion. It adopted and improved Roman techniques for arable and livestock agriculture, building, and trade and transport networks across Europe. Its heritage is much of what is today considered *civilisation*, monasteries, cathedrals, universities, libraries, law, education, music and art. Christianity became immensely successful, achieving political support for an exclusive faith, collecting a 10% tax, eventually controlling a third of Europe's property and the population's rites of passage from birth to death.

The christian Church attracted jealous antagonists. They sought to replace it, or at least to collect its taxes. The replacement organisation was almost identical to the original but, to pretend some difference, adopted the name of *protestant*. Its members needed to justify their decision to separate and to change their doctrine. They found support, once again, in the work of the Greek philosophers, who not only documented their conclusions about life and the human role in it, but also described their process of thought, logic and argumentation. These *humanists*, again put the human at the centre of affairs and stimulated the *renaissance*, literally rebirth, of critical thinking. It led to an explosion of discovery built on natural curiosity, as well as the wealth and leisure which now existed in middle- and upper-class families. It put the human being as an individual back in the centre; it ignored both divine intervention and mass organisation in the scheme of things.

Humanism led directly to attempts at scientific classification of nature. The most important action was to define the role of human beings in the nature of things. No longer was Man (and Woman) to be created at the end of a long week by an all-powerful deity. Instead, they created a pyramid of Nature, the base of which was the plant world, on which grazed the herbivores and frugivores, on whom preyed the carnivores and, above these as supreme ruler, sat *Homo sapiens*.

Humans had risen to control the natural pyramid through a combination of teamwork, preparation, training and special tools. However, human pride sought to ascribe its success to individuals and to specific and unique qualities. Early-modern philosophers decided that it was his intelligence that separated him from the wild beasts and made him king.

By the time that Carl Linnaeus started his monumental task of identifying every plant and animal species, intelligence was the preferred excuse for human superiority over beasts much bigger, heavier or stronger. Linnaeus granted the human species the binomial *Homo sapiens*. Listing the species within the order of primates, he was severely criticised, as these animals were clearly inferior to the lions and tigers, which Man had tamed.

Many naturalists who followed Linnaeus separated humans from the apes by creating orders for the bipedal versions, justifying it not so much on their form of locomotion as on their much greater intelligence.

Human intelligence could be measured by the size of the skull, and the human skull was much larger than that of any other primate, as well as much larger relative to its body size. However, lions and tigers have bigger heads. So, then the next step was to look at the brain size and, for extinct animals, the brain case. Humans have much bigger brains than lions and tigers.

Then, the intellectualists discovered that whales and elephants had much bigger brains, so they added ethics and culture to the debate. These abstract terms are impossible to quantify. It was equally clear that dolphins and whales, elephants and giraffes would be unable to compete in these arenas, not least because writing underwater is not easy and writing with hooves is not possible.

Microscopy introduced a new argument that permitted human superiority, as physiologists discovered that brains were made up neurons, and that the number of neurons depended on how the brain matter was folded up inside the brain case. Now, it did not matter who had the biggest brain, but the most folds and the most neurons. Humans had heavily-folded brains, and as they were the most intelligent creatures, and therefore superior to the rest of the planet wildlife, they must have more neurons, and more folds.

The latest theory to enter this debate is the ability of human intelligence to create imaginary ideas. *Sapiens* presents an idealistic view of the human species, in which intelligence plays the primordial role in its demographic and geographic success. In particular, Harari dwells on human capacity for cognitive dissonance and its support for the complex organisations of our civilisation, which he argues are necessary to provide the peace and certainty necessary for investment. [8]

As if the ambiguous and abstract ideas of the imagination were not enough to separate humans from beasts, the use of books, libraries, computers, Internet technology and artificial intelligence, has created the *extended mind*, a concept that excludes our closest competitors.

An Intellectual Framework

Throughout the thousands of years of documented philosophy, humans have modified the supposed purpose and achievement of human intelligence to meet temporal needs or fit into social acceptability.

In order to identify intelligence as the critical behaviour in the ascent of Man, or to refute the theory that it has played a major role, it is first necessary to define intelligence, its purpose and perhaps discover thereby its potential for achievement.

Intelligence can be defined as the ability for an identified entity to achieve specific (stated, observable, or measurable) objectives through the adaptation of

---

[8] No book in the field of human behaviour and evolution has had greater success since Darwin than *Sapiens* by Yuval Noah Harari, which has sold at least 12 Million copies. In comparison, the most influential science book of all time, according to the Royal Society 2017 poll, *The Selfish Gene*, by Richard Dawkins, sold barely a million copies.

behaviour under variable conditions and constraints. [9] The role of intelligence in a species would be paramount if it directly and uniquely led to its massive expansion in demographic and geographic terms. Conversely, if it does not have a major influence in demographic and geographic growth, then it is unlikely to be the most important characteristic of a species as promiscuously successful as *Homo sapiens*.

Intelligence is different to *competence*, which could be defined as the ability to carry out a predetermined action under specified circumstances. The difference would be that intelligence can deal with the unpredictable and still achieve success, whereas pure competence is only capable of repetitively achieving the same task.

Intelligence also needs separation from all the other many aspects of human behaviour and emotions that involve the brain. It makes no sense to lump together concepts such as self-awareness, bi-lingualism and colour vision in the term *intelligence*. They may all use the brain, but do not help to select a course of action that is beneficial for the human, a mate, children, neighbours, and the human's group and species.

Equally, it is important to recognise that intelligence and competence by themselves mean nothing. Humans can be both competent and intelligent,

---

[9] This is the author's definition, but not far removed from those of Alfred Binet, the inventor of intelligence testing. Wikipedia describes multiple concepts, which involve the observation or creation of information and its adaptive application as knowledge to problems. The throwaway comment that intelligence also exists in machines and even plants rather diminishes its allure.

but if they are lazy and fail to apply their gifts, then nothing will come of them. It is the application of intelligence and competence that leads to technological or process improvements, and these moments are rare, especially in political decision-making. Far more important in 2020 was personal survival and promotion.

If it is easy to measure intelligence in the classroom or laboratory, it is much harder to do so by observing the behaviour of individuals, and harder still if the observation is at second hand, or historical.

If, however, intelligence is defined as above, in terms of global population and expansion, it is possible to set specific objectives, and measure the outcomes of individuals' behaviour, or even of organisations' behaviour. Correlation of behaviour with results over multiple examples can provide an indication of whether intelligence is a driver for success.

For example, if national leaders can gain re-election by attacking their neighbours then it should be possible to measure this scientifically. Ample evidence exists to support the thesis that, consciously or sub-consciously, democratically-elected leaders seeking re-election attack other countries. There is a 50% greater chance of a president launching a war in an election year than in a normal year, regardless of the economic or social benefits accruing to the population. [10]

---

[10] The science is, inevitably for such a complicated subject, complicated. There is considerable variation depending on the situation of the incumbent, whether he is improving or decreasing in popularity, whether there is an improving or declining economy and whether external forces are leading to international conflict. See, for examples, [139]

If a national leader seeking re-election sees benefit in invading his neighbour, it does not necessarily follow that the tax-payers and citizens of his state will profit financially or in terms of longevity. There is no doubt that the decision is executed consciously, not least because of the involvement of others in communicating it. However, it is not clear that the decision-making process is conscious, or that the perpetrator is aware of the real reasons for the decision.

It remains to be seen whether war benefits mankind, the population of a territory at large or individuals. Clearly, many individuals benefit, if they survive, and some who die may also claim to have benefited in the time before their death or in their bequests. However, for the vast majority of those involved on both sides, war is a terrible and costly experience. Very few wars produce economic benefits for the species or the tax-payers that fund them. A few individuals may benefit, but rarely those who start them. [11]

War does permit, generally, an increase in taxation, through repression, censorship, and propaganda. This increase can result in benefits from improved transportation. One example would be air travel after the Second World War, which was much improved due to the many hardstanding airfields built, the personnel trained and the aircraft left over. Another benefit would come from the clearing of old city

----

[11] Napoleon Bonaparte, Napoleon III, the German kaiser and the Austrian emperor, Adolf Hitler, Neville Chamberlain and Édouard Daladier all failed to keep their jobs as a result of starting wars. Some were tried, convicted and imprisoned, others exiled, one died during the war and another fell on his sword.

centres, wooden warehouses like Silvertown, and the sinking of the last commercial sailing ships. [12]

Governments are not people, but they are made up by people, and their decisions are the result of interactions between them. Before anyone can criticise a government, organisation, politician or person for failure, the actual measure of success needs to be defined. Objectives are rarely defined in political circles, not least because those politicians who do define their objectives alienate many before approval and even more after failure; they rarely make it to the top of a hierarchical organisation.

Objective Intelligence

SMART objectives, where the letters spell out specific, measureable, agreed, realistic and timely, would form the basis of intelligent organisation. [13] However, most individuals do not consciously operate at this level, and will rarely admit to or describe their behaviour in these terms. In many cases, the working classes forced to work under these conditions for pin money, have rebelled. In spite of all the reports from scientific managers that clear objectives, good time

---

[12] Adolph Hitler was delighted, or at least claimed to be so, when the RAF started bombing German cities. He was well aware that their narrow streets prevented proper use of motor transport.

[13] Most users of SMART objectives, especially those set by superiors for the inferiors in hierarchical organisations, forget the A for *Agreed* and render it as *Achievable*, which makes no sense.

keeping and focus, will increase productivity, individuals prefer and will seek freedom to choose their own rhythm and avoid targets. At a simple level, therefore, the vast majority humans are not intelligent during their working day.

The logical failure is the absence of a measurable definition of intelligence, a SMART objective. Such a failure is common, and results in a process to define intelligence in such a way that humans come out on top. Such a process is always fraught with academic danger. All this is not to say that elephants and whales are more intelligent than humans, although their ability to survive *without tools*, in the water and on land is far superior to that of humans. It is unlikely that 99% of humans would survive for longer than a month without tools, or longer than a year without modern conveniences. Without first defining intelligence and its limits, it is impossible to have an intelligent discussion about it.

Ultimately, it is not what the brain might do but what it does that is important. Comparisons with other animals or fossil humans is relatively less important than analyses of human current behaviour and its use of the great potential intelligence provided by the brain. Few government leaders would claim high intelligence, and their decision-making processes prefer inclusivity and acceptance rather than brilliance. [14]   Voters

---

[14] Donald J. Trump has repeatedly claimed that he is "like, really smart", that he has a high IQ, is a "genius", and has a "very good brain". [158] His repeated attempts to convince others of his intelligence are reminiscent of human attempts to prove human intelligence.

similarly select based on sexual and emotional factors rather than cleverness. Perhaps the more intelligent candidates realise that being prime minister or president is not as appealing as the anonymity of some academic grove.

Objectives themselves are a source of argument. Freedom, liberty and honour are difficult to define. Protection, caring for the vulnerable, and public service are great ideals, and no rational human being could object to these objectives, but they are usually too abstract to benefit from clear definitions. Balancing the budget is perhaps more open to debate, less attractive to those who benefit from public spending, but easier to define and measure. Brexit was clear in the minds of those who voted for it but, apart from the application of article 50, few people can agree on what it means.

Once an objective is agreed by a group of people, claims of success or failure at its conclusion will depend on the measure of success chosen. If objectives are rarely stated clearly by those initiating action, clear measures of success are even rarer, for the same reason.

The reason for the difficulty in defining measures of success in such ideals as freedom and honour is that these terms are, first of all, nouns, and, secondly, abstract. Each person can have a pretty good idea of what these words mean to him or her, but he would be hard put to define it in measureable terms.

A measurable objective needs to have a quantifiable object or an observable behaviour. This excludes abstract nouns.

While porn stars, actors, writers and boxers are members of Mensa, few politicians and even fewer world leaders are.

Even some objectives that initially sound clear, vaporise on first contact with reality. The Brexit goal that no foreigner or unelected official should tell Brits what to do is perfectly reasonable to half the British population. However, those who understand how the British legal system works know that almost all British law is written by unelected judges. The most likely people to tell a Brexiteer what to do are unelected police and customs officials, while more unelected civil servants will take 20%, 40%, or more, of their wages without any negotiation at all. Britain is ruled by an unelected sovereign of basically German descent, the British head of government is of German-Turkish-Russian-Jewish-American descent, the British cabinet is dominated today by first generation Indian immigrants, including the richest MP married to one of the wealthiest women in the world, also Indian, and the mayor of London is a first generation immigrant from Pakistan. The minister appointed to deal with the COVID-19 vaccine, the second-richest MP, is a Kurd born in Iraq. The deputy chief medical officer responsible for COVID is of Vietnamese descent. The media in Britain, which has considerable power of lobby, is dominated by foreigners or tax-evading Britons. Britain has always been an attractive country and, since the last ice age, its green and pleasant land has welcomed waves of beaker folk, Celts, Romans, Angles, Jutes, Saxons, Danes, Norsemen, Normans, French, Flemings, Germans, Poles, Spaniards, Dutch, Indians, Africans, and Chinese. It is unlikely that any Brexiteer is descended from humans who somehow survived the Ice Age while living in Britain. All are immigrants or sons or daughters of immigrants.

In addition, the political pressure exerted on British policy by the United States, by the various lobbies of foreign interests, and by the City of London, by foreign owners of British debt, and by the only likely buyers of Britain's future COVID debt, as well as by certain industrial sectors such as energy and water, dominated by foreign firms, and arms, totally dependent on foreign buyers, means that elected officials British-born of British parents wield little power.

In this case, the easily observable and quantifiable objective of freedom from foreign rulers is not achieved at present, nor is it likely to be achieved any time in the future. Freedom from foreign rule could only be achieved anywhere in the world by a form of autarky and isolation that would collapse a modern economy, with an inevitable fall in the population and the quality of life.

Freedom is often part of or the sole demand of political activists. A reasonable objective for freedom could be freedom from exploitative taxation, in other words, that all taxes raised are spent on and in the local community. City taxes are spent in the city, state taxes in the state, and national or federal taxes benefit the whole country. [15] There is no rationale for expenditure in foreign tax territories that a tax-payer would accept. This would avoid foreign wars, pork belly politics, and vanity projects.

---

[15] This freedom formed part of the negotiations between the English Crown and the rebellious barons, which led to the Magna Carta. The result was a confirmation that taxes raised in England, including military service, should be spent in England, and not on foreign wars.

However, there is no such thing as freedom from foreign interference in a country with foreign relations. All such relations depend on bilateral agreement, hundreds of them in modern society, in which the other party or parties does interfere. The only other relationship is a colonial one, in which military force is used to impose one-sided conditions, with no obligation in return. Britain and European nations have few such relationships available. France attempts to maintain its hold on the uranium mines of the Sahara in this way, but Britain is now incapable of managing even this on its own. The USA, with Britain as its bagman, can control the finances of Iraq, but has never managed to do so in Afghanistan.

The Dumb Ape

No one is more hated than he who speaks the truth [16]

If self-definition is a uniquely-human habit, so is self-delusion. The myth that humans are intelligent is best disproved by human behaviour. This is particularly true of behaviour towards those who are seen as intellectual.

The Conundrum of Stupid Behaviour

Not all intelligent behaviour is a good idea. Telling people the truth is rarely a good idea, even when they ask for it. It can result in a beating, a prison sentence or a divorce.

If some intelligent behaviour has a negative effect on a country's economy and demography, there is no doubt that some human behaviour is plain stupid. This also raises a question about the very existence of stupidity; if it is detrimental to species survival, why does it still exist, why has it not evolved out ? Why do lemmings jump off cliffs, why do dolphins and whales swim onto beaches ?

Intelligence has a place in human life, it has created wonderful examples, works of art, buildings, technology and literature. However, its proponents provide little evidence that it has impact on population

---

[16] Plato, from the *Socratic Dialogues*.

growth and the economy that supports it. [17]   More interestingly, they avoid any discussion of the stupidity and incompetence that characterises most human behaviour.

Human behaviour in relation to the environment, climate change, Brexit, COVID and the latest experience in the United States under President Donald J. Trump show that, even in those countries that have the greatest freedom to use their intelligence, with the easiest access to education systems capable of leveraging that intelligence into productive outcomes, about half the population is completely wrong about the most important subjects, and maybe the entire population is wrong. Not only is its intellectual decision-making capacity faulty, but its decisions actually cause the opposite of what it seeks.

There are many books already written on these subjects and there will be many more. The most erudite and disinterested works have been largely ignored, while partisan polemics sell widely. The reaction to intelligent works on these subjects mirrors the behaviour of humans. In the recent elections in the United States, 2016 and 2020, the intelligent libertarian party scored 1% of the vote. In the Brexit referendum vote, 28% of voters refused to vote, while the large majority voted almost equally for the two options presented, neither of which made any sense.

It is not the purpose of this book to look at the arguments for and against Brexit or Trump, government

---

[17] In many cases, from rich-men's follies through corporate headquarters and royal palaces, they show a lack of intelligence.

measures during the COVID panic, or indeed other subjects of the political arena, climate change, the environment or pollution. However, for those interested who can't be bothered to read another book, the author includes the intelligent version of each of these fiascos in appendices at the end.

There are many other examples of stupid human behaviour. These extend from simple belief systems such as religion, through pseudo-scientific ones such as homeopathy, which may include some scientifically-observable benefits due to the placebo effect, to outright disasters such as communism and cults, climate change and the environment. Individuals participate in dangerous activities, often to avoid mate selection opportunities, otherwise the only genetic reason for such participation. Intelligent people promote and support species-ending social behaviours, such as homosexuality and family planning, with the inevitably-resulting invasion by foreign hordes, rape and murder.

In 2020, governments have failed to deal successfully with the coronavirus pandemic. With a few exceptions, governments have closed their borders, destroying the inward investment of tourism dollars and the money-saving and life-saving of new technology. Governments have closed hotels and restaurants, wiping out investments and rendering the workers unemployed. Border closures have done nothing to prevent infection and reinfection, or the arrival of terrorists.

In Britain, the government had to deal with COVID and with the self-inflicted catastrophe of Brexit. Instead of using COVID as an excuse to stop Brexit, it doubled up and inflicted another rack of harm to its bewildered economy.

Other western nations, avoiding Brexit, succumbed to the temptation provided by COVID. The result of government action, supported by a wide variety of non-governmental and commercial organisations, has been a collapse in the global economy, mass closure of businesses and vastly increased unemployment, only partially hidden by a variety of *furlough* schemes designed to delay unemployment until a new politician takes over.

Democratic countries have implemented policies only seen in peacetime in authoritarian dictatorships or police states. [18] The public, meanwhile, who should resist this affront on liberties fought for over centuries, acquiesced silently, or no more vociferously than for actions against petrol tax increases (France, yellow vests), or police brutality (Nigeria, Chile, Hong Kong, USA black lives matter).

There is nothing new about disastrous decisions from government. The destruction of every empire in history can be ascribed to idiotic decisions made by emperors and their closest advisors. The British Empire was only the last empire to collapse as the result of poor decision making. Certainly, a more intelligent decision than starting a war that killed 60 Million people and whose sole benefit was a fleet of aeroplanes and the

---

[18] Even the Nazi German occupation forces in France and Italy did not implement such draconian lockdowns as those by France's conservative president and by Italy's highly intelligent prime minister, both of whom ignored democratic means and ruled mostly by decree. Both suffered severe economic downturns. Both are major tourist destinations, Paris is the global capital of tourism and the centre of the luxury goods trade, the ultimate non-essential business. It is unlikely that both will recover for five years.

airports to provide a global service would have been to remain at peace and use normal taxes to build passenger airlines, public airports and rebuild cities. It is, however, unlikely that such a large investment in technology and infrastructure as occurred during the war would have been possible in peacetime. The political obstacles to such improvement again show that intelligence is rarely the cause of human civilisation, but the accident of human stupidity. However, the cost of destroyed infrastructure, and the obsession of Polish and German citizens with rebuilding their old towns exactly as they were before the war, wasted much of the opportunity for improvement provided by the war.

If the destruction of the British Empire can be ascribed to idiotic decisions by its political leaders, there is no evidence to suggest that its creation was the result of intelligent behaviour, either. It was not the result of a planned, rational decision, or even of a series of such decisions, carefully calculated to create a major imperial force. It was certainly the result of aggressive, acquisitive and exploitative instincts, backed up or caused by an accidentally-high population growth.

The idiocy of government behaviour is obvious to many distant observers, but not to those closely involved in the processes. Nor does stupidity explain the reason for its ubiquity, its evolutionary survival, nor the difficulty in executing more sensible alternatives. Perhaps there is another explanation.

A few countries managed the COVID crisis well, but even some of those cracked and implemented the fatal trio of lockdown, mask and fines. Britain started off refusing this easy option, but also ignored the important virus identification part of the WHO recommendations. The USA ignored the virus at a federal (national) level, but then implemented lockdowns and masks locally.

Life in lockdown in 2020 involved being forced to show a travel permit to leave the house, to wear a mask at all times in public places, seeing queues to buy food, shortages of basic necessities, children left without school, old age pensioners abandoned in don't-care homes, patients on trolleys in corridors or even in hospital car parks for lack of attention, bodies in sheets lined up for communal burial. Modern historians can only reflect on the zero progress made from the moral mire of 1930s fascism, or the confused communism of the 1950s. What is seen in colour is little different to the black and white representations of earlier times, of a film noir, or horror flick. This impression is increased by the tunnel vision of hand-held media showing night-time scenes of the resistance, poorly equipped young men facing the Gestapo and Stasi, the Stormtroopers, the tanks, their futile gestures poetic and hopeful, ghostly images filtered by smoke and gas, vibrating with shock and panic, communicating their fear through curses and screams of pain.

The Evolution of Intelligence

Nobody likes a smart Alec. [19] This universal truth should be enough to refute any theory that

---

[19] Rendered vulgarly in the USA as *smart a*s*, and in Britain as *smart a**e*. The earl of Stafford once said "seeing a man reading a book makes me want to draw my sword". The duke of

intelligence has played a major role in the population growth of the human species. However, there is additional evidence that can help to refute the theory that intelligence plays the major role in human population success.

Members of the species *Homo sapiens* are intelligent. Some are perhaps more intelligent, and others less; some are inexperienced, especially the isolated, the young and the old, while others have the wisdom of experience. However, that does not provide a causal relationship for the success of the human species in terms of its geographic and demographic expansion.

Intelligence can be considered the ability to think for oneself, to use one's intelligence to decide on a course of action, ignoring evolution, peer-pressure and the environment, or to not think for oneself, to obey the prescriptions of a selected guru or group, to follow training or upbringing, to save the brain for more important work. In both cases, the perpetrator can seek a personal, group or species advantage. Both have some claims, and human history shows that both ideas exist, sometimes simultaneously. However, the existence of some kind of intelligence does not make it the cause of human success. Nor does it seem likely that polar opposites could both be a suitable process for decision making. One is associated with a heavy survival cost, while the other's inflexible approach to changing

---

Gloucester said "another damned, thick, square book, eh, Mr Gibbons?" on the publication of *The Decline and Fall of the Roman Empire*. The English upper classes refused to talk to engineers, or even to sit in the same carriage. The Corinthian attitude extended to military adventures, exploration, and mountaineering.

circumstances opposes it to the general idea that human adaptability is responsible for much of human success.

Biblical Intelligence

As a story to describe human evolution, the Bible lacks any empathy and makes no claim for the species; part of its importance is the justification for taxation while encouraging or at least acquiescing to any crime against foreigners and heretics. The key books are the Mosaic ones, listing not just the Ten Commandments, but an entire book of laws, taxes and obedience to the priests. It glorifies the low cunning of Jacob, Joseph and David, and finds Solomon's rather banal judgements worthy of praise, when they are more fitted to a Men-Only Club's comedy night. [20] David's artistic talent as the author of the Psalms is mediocre at

---

[20] Solomon no doubt benefitted from the temporary weakness of his major neighbours in Egypt, Anatolia and Mesopotamia, and the propensity of his entourage to furnish him with daughters in exchange for preferment or patronage. Although Solomon benefitted personally, patronage is a euphemism for tax cuts for the rich. Clearly, the tax-payer and consumer must have suffered as a result. The girls themselves, after the initial fascination with a rich and powerful (old) man, the luxury of the harem, and the temporary possession of dowry, jewels and clothes, must have found life as one of a thousand concubines dreary. They were never wives. Raising children, one every three years, in a healthy environment would have provided some escape and an evolutionary advantage. After Solomon squandered Israel's wealth on such luxury, his heirs suffered civil war, conquest and slavery. However intelligent Solomon was, it is hardly intelligent behaviour to praise such a national leader.

best, and only remarkable for his work's survival across three thousand years.

Although God promised Abraham that his descendants would number like the stars in the heavens, it is not clear that he kept his promise. Self-identifying Jews still only number a few million, while there are a billion trillion stars visible, at least with a telescope. The rest of the human population has certainly expanded but, to their chagrin, the Jews for all their wisdom permitted the rise of a much more successful competitor.

The Hebrew Bible formed the documentary basis for a new religion, that of Christianity. Although successful economically, the members of the Church suffered from internal rules demanding chastity. This hardly helped the Catholic gene survive. The Catholic Church was in many places replaced by the more virile protestant one, which held no such scruples and allowed its staff the freedom to fornicate, if within marriage. Protestant territories outperformed their Catholic competitors and defeated them in successive battles. The protestant empires replaced the catholic ones around the world.

Protestantism carried the seed of science. It held human experience superior to that communicated by priests through translated books. That at least represented a minor triumph for intelligence. However, humanism also carried the flawed idea that a benevolent tyrant was the best form of government. This idea had its origins in the first great humanist, the inventor of the term, Cicero, a Roman orator, lawyer and politician. Petrarch's adoration of Cicero derived from the latter's writings, beautiful prose and idyllic imaginings of human behaviour, but ignored his brutality, ambition and his cruel execution by a lynch mob. Whatever the benefits of a benevolent tyrant, and there can be many, they don't survive much beyond his senility or death, and rarely much beyond the first few years of his power. The very real danger of supporting a tyrant, any tyrant, is that whoever succeeds him will be a despot without any of the redeeming characteristics so attractive in an absolute ruler. Every Julius Caesar is followed by a Caligula, but even Caesar had his bad days, murdering Vercingetorix and thousands of Gauls to celebrate his triumph, embarrass Pompey and sway the plebs. Caesar's clemency was second only to that of Titus, but he killed tens of thousands of Spaniards, Gauls, Britons, Belgians and Germans to gain absolute power, while sparing the lives of only a few Romans to gain the honour of a temple to his *clementia*.

Julius Caesar was the first European celebrity superstar.   Rather than dwell on the teamwork, preparation, training and special tools necessary for the engineering marvels of the age, which Caesar used to achieve his otherwise almost miraculous conquests, the population preferred to adulate the human and ascribe divine nature. The stupidity of such behaviour became evident as future generations showed no ability to manage the opportunities and resources of state, and degenerated into an orgy of self-gratification and waste only partially alleviated by the occasional massacre by the Praetorian Guard. Caligula and Nero were only the most famous of the bad leaders of Rome, but there were four bad ones for every good one, hardly a successful result for the intelligent ape.

Although there was a strong movement to give importance to intelligence in the natural classification of Linnaeus and others who followed him, there were others who considered it merely a minor adaptation to ecological niches. For Darwin, "the comparative insignificance for classification of the great development of the brain in man" was no more important than those adaptations of Galapagos tortoises to the different habitat on their different islands.

Even before Darwin published the first of his influential works, *The Origin of Species*, in 1859, palaeontologists had discovered the first skeletons of Neanderthal Man. Neanderthal's head was huge, and his brain cavity much bigger than the average human's. First interpretations rendered him an above average human, but his primitive features, powerful body, large teeth, and prognathous jaw became apparent as more and more skeletons were discovered in the bone mania of the late 19th and early 20th Century. With the general acceptance of Darwin's theories of natural selection, the world was prepared to accept that humans descended from apes in a form of natural progression, but they were not yet prepared to accept that humans were not the most intelligent ape to have existed.

Darwin himself wrote that domestication, with all its attendant advantages, rendered intelligence less useful, and would evolve out of the species.   He had already observed that domesticated animals, such as cats and dogs, sheep and cows, were less intelligent than their wild cousins. He considered that humans were merely the domesticated primate, less intelligent than the last wild hominid. This idea has never been popular.

Scientists still believed in the primacy of intelligence to explain or justify human superiority and the treatment of other animals. With the appearance of new evidence for evolution and the confusion provided by Neanderthals bones, intellectualists developed increasingly scientific approaches to attempt to prove their point of view. At each stage they found that human uniqueness or superiority existed only in imagination. Head size, brain case size, number of neurons, number of brain neurons, were all put under the microscope. If comparisons with extant primates produced positive results, they failed when extended to the fossils of Neanderthals, or to other mammals like elephants and whales.

Attempts to sideline the fossil evidence with recourse to abstract concepts like ethics and culture are hardly scientific and, in spite of repetition, proponents of this behavioural adaptation still fail to prove its value.

Microscopy introduced a new argument, as physiologists discovered that brains were made up neurons, and that the number of neurons depended on how the brain matter was folded up inside the brain case. Now, it did not matter who had the biggest brain, but the most folds, and the most neurons. Humans had heavily-folded brains, and as they were the most intelligent creatures, and therefore superior to the rest of the planet wildlife, they must have more neurons, and more folds.

Humans could reign supreme, at least for a while. This new theory lasted only as long as it took naturalists to study the neurons and brains of other animals under a microscope. They discovered that other living animals had neurons just as numerous as humans. The dolphin, a mammal about the same size and weight as a human, has a similar sized brain, while an elephant's brain is much larger and can have three times the number of neurons. Whales' brains are even larger.

Apologists for human intelligence started again. They looked at human culture and decided that language was the unique feature that differentiated us from the savage beasts. This language was what permitted our culture to develop, and showed the moral principles of good and evil. Animals simply had nothing to show in comparison.

However, animal language is adequate for its needs. Human inability to interpret it is not proof of its simplicity. Western colonialists disparaged Asiatic languages and culture, until they discovered a much richer history and variety. The difficulty for Europeans of learning African click language or Asian phonetic ones hides their subtleties and culture.

The part of the brain responsible for language is the neocortex. Humans have a particularly large neocortex. For a time, the neocorticists triumphed, creating a wodge of papers to prove human superiority through arcane regions of the brain. Inevitably, as with any pseudo-religious belief, there came the Fall, as those with access to the tree of knowledge eventually traced the pilot whale. This small whale has a neocortex that is even bigger than that of humans, but has failed to produce a viable civilisation. Why a pilot whale should need such a brain is difficult to imagine, as is what it does with so much intelligence. One thing that it does do is occupy in large numbers all the oceans of the world.

Even then, these pseudo-scientific theories appealed more to males than to their smaller-brained female colleagues, and to the younger rather than to the older ones, whose neurons disappear 1 for every second of their lives.   Any older person knows that they know far more than a younger person, with more neurons, a larger and more functional neocortex. Intelligence has little to do with the size of the brain, and achievement has little to do with intelligence.

Even those animals with smaller brains, smaller neocortices, less neurons, like the chimpanzee, can perform some intellectual tasks better than humans. It appears that chimps can identify their environment with a precision which atrophied humans living in civilisation for thousands of years, have long since lost. This kind of active intelligence is perhaps more to do with the stimulation and development of the environment and peer-pressure rather than the innate capacity of the brain.

Every attempt by scientists to prove that human uniqueness stems from greater intelligence fails because by every measure selected, the dumb beasts are better. The latest attempts ascribe intelligence to "a combination of the number of cortical neurons, neuron packing density, interneuronal distance and axonal conduction velocity", giving, as a product of their multiplication, information processing capacity (IPC). [21] Against other mammals, humans do well with this classification, beating the elephants and whales. However, the crows and parrots, with much smaller brains, do just as well.

Scientific attempts to understand intelligence fail because of the inevitable assumption that humans

---

[21] [159]

are the most intelligent creatures. Having made this assumption, it follows that what humans do is intelligence, and what animals do is not, or is at least a lesser form. This logic, starting from a false assumption, leads to ridiculous and embarrassing results, and comments that humans are more intelligent than elephants and whales "without any doubt". [22] Doubt is the starting point of any scientific process; without it there is faith, the enemy of science.

The Clever Monkey

Homo sapiens is a species of ape, one of many mammals that inhabit the Earth. [23] It is the only ape that has achieved global coverage, and only other species of the genus *Homo* have ever existed on two continents. [24]

Homo sapiens is likely the primate with the largest-ever population. Previous *Homo* species have also outperformed all other primate species. However,

---

[22] [159]

[23] *Homo sapiens* is the sole extant species of the *genus Homo*; all other *Homo* species are now extinct. Species in this context means that any two humans could produce fertile offspring, assuming that they meet other conditions as well. The *family Hominidae*, the *hominids*, includes our great ape cousins, the chimpanzees, gorillas and orangutans. The *superfamily* of *hominoids* includes the lesser apes, the gibbons. The *order* of *primates* includes the Old World (Asia & Africa) and New World (America) monkeys. Primates are in the *class* of *mammals*, in the animal *kingdom*. These *taxa* include all extinct and extant species, families and orders.

[24] Human ancestor *Homo erectus* roamed Africa and Eurasia.

there is little evidence that intelligence had much to do with this.

The most intelligent primate was *Homo neanderthalensis*, as measured in its brain capacity. [25] Neanderthal Man was stronger and more intelligent than *Homo sapiens,* yet was wiped out in little more than 20,000 years by his younger, weaker and less intelligent competitor.

The remaining apes and primates survive in deep jungle, but as this is cut up by *Homo sapiens*, their populations diminish. The surviving primate populations, in spite of their much greater intelligence than neighbouring herbivores, struggle to maintain their population. They suffer from the difficult conditions of human predation and habitat destruction, but also benefit from the much greater predator destruction of humans. Intelligence should aid in adaptation to changing circumstances, according to the theories, but doesn't help in practice.

The largest non-human population of primates consists of macaques. These are followed by gibbons and geladas. All three are ahead of chimpanzees and gorillas. The population of equally-intelligent bonobos is a quarter or less of the chimpanzees. Population has much more to do with suitable ecological niche.

Almost all primates are endangered. This is in spite of their intelligence, by far the highest of any order of terrestrial animals. Gorillas and chimpanzees seem

---

[25] It could be argued that some modern humans have larger brains than the average Neanderthal; however, it would generally be accepted that Neanderthals were at least as intelligent as humans, certainly not less.

to survive more because of their size than their intelligence. Again, there is little difference in intelligence between chimpanzees and bonobos, and between western and eastern gorillas, but there are orders of magnitude difference in population.

If it is not intelligence that makes primates grow their population or expand into other territories, then an alternative behavioural explanation is needed to explain human expansion across Africa, across rivers, across deserts, and out of Africa, across seas, mountains and against existing populations of hominids, primates, and predators.

It is difficult to compare populations of extinct mammal species with those of living creatures. Species are defined by their ability to procreate successfully and produce fertile offspring, while for fossils, the only requirement is for anatomical correlation. Even so, extinct and living primate species have failed to migrate fast enough or successfully enough to maintain the species across long-distance migration. Only humans have done this, and the latest generation of not very smart human is the most successful of all.

Those humans who migrate are not likely to be the most successful, or the strongest. They may have been the most intelligent, shy, sensitive types who could not resist the banter and bullying normal in any primate community. Even today, villages are dominated by the strongest bully, not the most intelligent, leading to rural intellectual atrophy and urban pansification.

If intelligence had little to do with human expansion and population growth, there is even less evidence that it has improved as the world has become more complicated. The opposite appears to be the case.

As humans moved from monoface to biface to complex tool assemblages to polishing stones, their brains atrophied. Similarly, as political constructs became more complicated, brains got smaller. It is easier to survive, even to complete IQ tests, as a result of the increasing complexity of life support systems, such as vaccination, antibiotics, universal healthcare, guaranteed education, unemployment protection and obligatory pensions.

Relative Importance of Intelligence

Even if intelligence exists and humans have more of it than other animals, it is questionable whether intelligence, as conscious or unconscious problem-solving ability, is the most important aspect of life. 99% of human behaviour is not intelligent, it is just reaction to circumstances.

Humans, like all living organisms, are made up of cells. Cell birth, operation and self-destruction is a marvellous, almost miraculous, process, still unknown to the majority of the human population. The single cell of a unicellular organism may have no brain, and is therefore theoretically incapable of learning and solving complex problems, such as how to deal with the human immune system. However, viruses and bacteria as species are perfectly capable of mutating to overcome such defences, and even mutating to stimulate behaviour to weaken it. This racial intelligence operates across generations and cell boundaries, in the same way that human intelligence relies on computers and the Internet to solve problems in the extended mind.

As well as its own cells, human bodies consist of billions, at least a similar number, of parasitical cells, viruses, bacteria, fungi, archaea, and protists. Through the simple process of natural selection, these foreign invaders perform essential functions for human survival. They help in signalling for mate selection and violence avoidance. They defend the body from pathogens, digest food, and dissolve waste.

Humans could survive without these single-cell organisms, but there is no doubt that they have made themselves at home in the body. It is questionable whether they are any less part of the body than any of the other cells which carry human DNA. It would make sense to consider humans as a mutualistic organism, like lichen or mycorrhiza.

The processes that involve these visitors control or modify are carried through without human thought or intervention, apart from the odd deliberate dose of yoghurt or the accidental destruction of the gut biota with antibiotics. Intelligence has played little part in this interesting, if only recently understood, half of the human body.

While pathogenic micro-organisms stimulate the human body's immune defences, commensal microbiota do not, at least not while they remain in equilibrium with the rest of the microbiome. It is not clear why this happens, however it could be one reason for the strange effects of vaccination. Whereas live and attenuated live vaccines produce powerful immune responses, killed or inactivated vaccines have much weaker effects, and may lead to weaker immune responses to actual pathogens. [26] Again, although there appears to be some opportunity for human intervention through *positive thinking*, most immune reactions are autonomic.

At a larger, multicellular level, the human body again operates without conscious thought. The kidneys, for example, clean the blood without needing further input. They are autonomous by design. On the other hand, they are intelligent enough to process data from the brain and central nervous system, and pass

---

[26] [161]

information from one kidney to another, for example to regulate sodium levels. This intelligence, however, is pre-programmed. A kidney is not able to learn new tricks, neither to destroy a stone nor to clean the blood stream of some new parasite or poison that is killing it. Any intelligence ascribed to its function operates at an evolutionary level of hundreds or thousands of years.

More complicated organs, like the central nervous system, the skin, the cardio-vascular system, and the brain with its auricular and optical sensors, also work quite happily without any conscious interference. For a third of the day, the human relaxes unconscious. Major human organs continue to function normally in a comatose person, if not otherwise injured. Science-fiction stories of journeys to Outer Space depend on human ability to survive extended hibernation.

Humans have a limited conscious control of their ingestion, but whether they use their left hand or their right hand for eating soup is usually determined by their genes. Digestion in the stomach is automatic, the production of acid and enzymes, the churning, the opening and closing of the lower oesophageal and the pyloric sphincters, peristalsis in the intestines progresses with predictable regularity. Attempts to prevent defecation through intellectual determinism may be successful for a short period, but fail dramatically after a while.

In general, the human ability to consciously decide a course of action is possible only for a little while. During this time, conscious effort is necessary to limit the body's natural abilities to take care of itself. A slip of consciousness, the loss of will-power, results in autonomic action. A drowning man can hold his breath underwater, but only for a minute or two. [27] Any need for action, swimming, or fighting with another, will reduce this time. While under water, even knowing intellectually that breathing in will cause his death, a drowning man will eventually open his mouth and breathe in. Having made an intellectual decision to die, the drowning man will still fail to prevent the autonomic reaction of laryngospasm, in which the voice box resists the water entry.

Some instincts are so subtle that in normal life they are undetectable. Many children have played in the bath, trying to hold their breath for as long as possible. Much rarer is the need to avoid drinking water. Water is either available or not, and the body does an excellent job of forcing itself to drink when needed, to maintain a perfect balance of sodium and water in its cells. One curious case arises when the only water that is available is highly concentrated in sodium. After two or three days in an open lifeboat at sea, thirst drives the human to seek relief by drinking sea-water. This is further proof that intelligence is a weak force in human survival. Even knowing that drinking sea-water is fatal, people still do it. This may be an unfair example, as few members of a lifeboat participate.

Locomotion is another unconscious, unintelligent act. While the brain may engage to decide on a destination, and even select an appropriate mode of transport, the latter decision is more a justification for

---

[27] Breath-hold time decreases rapidly with water temperature, and below 15°C is a matter of seconds. The diving response helps most mammals reduce their oxygen consumption when under cold water. Both these sometimes conflicting reactions are autonomic. [166]

taking a preferred mode than a conscious internal argument. Rarely do people engage in a mechanical cost-benefit analysis of the various options, nor do they select the measures in advance, and stick to the result regardless.

The only behaviour that requires conscious or unconscious problem solving skills is thinking. Thinking about thinking is rarely conscious, almost all work using intelligence is unconscious.

The popular view of human intelligence is at odds with a scientific definition. Humans started defining intelligence as conscious thought, self-awareness, looking neither at the process nor the result. After thousands of years of argument, the only definition that survives is the innate, genetic one of unconscious thought. This capacity may be greater in humans, with the advantage of hands and tools, than in other animals, but a true scientific test would measure such intelligence in conditions of equality. It is unlikely that a two-year old child would beat a two-year old chimpanzee or elephant in finding food or water in a forest, or a two year old whale in finding fish in the sea; equally, it is unlikely that a 30-year old male gorilla would find food in an urban environment without alerting the authorities.

Finally, on death, the human microbiome takes over, rapidly become its necrobiome. Again, innate intelligence, evolved over millennia, reduces the human body to a feast for Mother Nature. In a matter of days, the carcass is ready for disposal by a million different organisms. Whatever intelligence existed, the body's ability to solve new problems dissolves with its integrity.

Intelligence "can be understood as mental or behavioural flexibility or the ability of an organism to solve problems occurring in its natural and social environment, culminating in the appearance of novel solutions that are not part of the animal's normal repertoire." [28] This behaviour is a rarity in human terms. Few humans show this behaviour, and those that do, do so rarely. Most of the cellular, organic and corporal behaviour is unconscious and most behaviour does not use intelligence.

The rare occasions when intelligence is necessary, a rock-climber learning a new move, a mathematician creating a new theory, a writer preparing a new book, the experience is so painful that it is often not attempted again. However, repetition of something already learnt the first time causes none of the pain of the learning experience. Equally, copying another rock climber who has just found the right move is also much less painful. Copying, however, is not inventing.

Even so, academics and popular writers continue to propose intelligence in some form or other as responsible for human success, and they support their hypotheses with the evidence of culture and civilisation.

---

[28] According to "the majority of behaviourists and animal psychologists", as summarised in [160]. This is also a good definition for the purpose of evolution.

Population success of other animals compared to humans and intelligence

Outside primates, other mammals have been successful in evolutionary terms, expanding in population and geography. Again, intelligence plays little part in their success.

Whales and dolphins are the most intelligent mammals after primates, and have an oceanic range second only to sea-birds. Their populations rise and fall with the availability of krill and other prey, and the attraction of their blubber, not with variations in their intelligence. In the case of the sperm whale, its spermaceti is highly attractive, but it seems not so much related to its intelligence as to its buoyancy. Overall, there seems little correlation between intelligence and population. Far more successful than whales and dolphins, krill are mostly eaten during the year, but their total biomass, made up of 85 species, is far greater. Each species of krill has on average four trillion individuals alive at one time, far more than any mammal. Krill are hardly the most intelligent of animals, not even the most intelligent of crustaceans.

Dogs and cats are highly successful mammals, but have become so only in their dumb and domesticated versions, smaller, weaker and less intelligent than their wild cousins. Domestication in all animals, including human, leads to a diminishing requirement for intelligence, and the result is smaller brains. Civilisation is not the result of great intelligence, but the cause of decline.

Livestock follows the same pattern. Cattle, sheep and goats are numerous. Cattle number over a billion and, due to their size, exceed humans in biomass. Sheep and goats are smaller but more numerous, approaching humans in biomass. The billions of cattle, sheep and goats have also experienced the atrophy of their most prized organs, being generally more appreciated for their meat than their brains, although sheep brains are a delicacy. The result of this process, however, is the largest population of mammals on the planet.

The only large animals that outnumber these farm animals are chickens, with about 10 billion alive at any one time. Their intelligence is so small that they are able to run about even after their heads are chopped off. Mike the Headless Chicken survived for 18 months, far longer than a broiler would normally live. [29]

What is it that prevents chimpanzees from doing what humans do ? Is it bipedalism ? Is it a small brain ? Under human training, chimpanzees can learn to communicate with humans (that is, learn a foreign language, for they already communicate among themselves), fashion tools better than the twigs and spears they already use, and co-operate to hunt. Left to themselves, they could evolve over the next million years the vocal chords and palate to enable full speech, a larger brain to take advantage of the possibilities, and representative democracy.

However, this scenario from *Planet of the Apes* is unlikely; chimpanzees have not taken the first step on the road to civilisation, and do not look like doing so.

---

[29] Humans cannot run far having lost their heads, although many humans continue to function after losing part or all of their brain. [164]

In spite of all the training in labs and zoos, chimpanzees are still chimpanzees. Their behaviour has not changed. They are not capable of defending themselves against the most aggressive predator on the planet, *Homo sapiens*. Their jungle habitat is under threat, not just from bushmeat merchants but from loggers, tourists, hunters and a human population infected with a wide range of diseases and parasites that co-habit in chimpanzees. In order to defend their territory against well-organised humans, they would have to combine with other groups. This they are not able to do. The first evolutionary step needs to be to inhibit their natural aggression towards other groups.

In the same way, human behaviour has not changed for thousands of years, and neither the increase in intelligence nor the decrease in intelligence has made much difference. Humans are humans, not because of bipedality or intelligence, tool use or sweating skin, but because of some behavioural constant that might use these and surpasses them all in importance, such that neither ecological disaster nor predation affect its success, and geographic barriers for other animals become opportunities.

Refutation of intelligence

However, there is no evidence for and much evidence against the claim that intelligence itself is directly responsible for the growth of the human population now numbers in the billions.

Humans did evolve intelligence, and used it to expand throughout Africa, Europe, Asia and even Australasia. The latest and now sole surviving human species possesses great intelligence and also expanded widely. However, for most of the two hundred thousand years of *Homo sapiens'* existence, its population remained no greater than that of any other large mammal, and its expansion was equalled by lions, hyenas and wolves, all animals of much lesser intelligence, none of which have attracted any scientific claims that they possess an ability to think in abstract terms.

Only in the last twenty thousand years, and really only in the last twelve or even ten thousand years, has human population exploded, has the species created the civilisation of which it is so proud. Yet its intelligence has not significantly changed over the species' existence. Therefore, intelligence is not the cause of this population growth. Whatever led to the agricultural revolution, it was not an increase in intelligence, nor was it the existence of intelligence.

Any animal can evolve greater intelligence. Most mammals will produce a variety of intelligence in each succeeding generation but few show any signs of this as a natural adaptation. Human efforts at genetic manipulation through livestock breeding have resulted in lower intelligence, while human effect on wild animals has been to make them more timorous, not more intelligent. There is no correlation between the intelligence of a mammal species and its population. Some of the dumbest animals have the largest populations, while the most intelligent are often scarce. Mammal species' population fluctuates wildly with food availability, not with increasing intelligence. The population also fluctuates with human predation.

Human population, when divided into groups, geographic, national, religious, or cultural, also show no correlation with intelligence. Humans are on average equally intelligent around the world, yet there is a wide difference in population growth rates, and there has been throughout history.

Misoverestimating Government

In order to understand the specific human behaviour that permits numerous groups of unknowns to co-operate, it is worth looking at specific examples of human behaviour. The recent behaviour of governments, many of whom behaved in similar ways under a single pressure, is a good opportunity.

However, it is important to separate human behaviour from political propaganda. The difference is that politicians rarely take responsibility for their actions. They blame others and claim merely to react. They claim privilege. They euphemise and use abstract terminology to prevent measurable and meaningful criticism; in other words, they avoid scientific process.

The confusion created by a government's own communication means that it should be ignored. The only valuable evidence is provided by direct observation, for which there is plenty, thanks to politicians' delight of the media spotlight.

Politicians are not evil, nor are they dumb. They are not benevolent, nor are they intelligent. Sometimes, their actions grant benefits to their friends, sometime to their enemies. Sometimes, they hurt those who support them, who vote for them, sometimes they do things that are initially criticised, and then later accepted by all as great and good. Often, propaganda and the press cover up the mistakes and the benefits, and leave only a false image, a fake history behind.

Politicians are no different to journalists, or almost anybody else, in that their principal objective is to keep their job and, if they can do that, to climb the hierarchy of their chosen career and reach the top.

The biggest problem, however, is not that politicians are evil or stupid, or even that they are clever or benevolent, but that they are misunderstood.

The ideal of government

All mammals look for protection, comfort and leadership from their parents, their group, and their masters. Harlow's appalling experiments on monkeys showed the terrifying psychological effect on monkeys that he deprived of leadership, guidance, comfort and, above all, protection. Neotenation has increased human need for governance and extended it throughout adulthood.

Humans find leadership in their immediate family, especially in patriarchal or matriarchal societies. They can find leadership in religion, industry, political parties, sport and hobbies, schools and above all, in government.

In the unconscious human mind, government is the resource of protection, moral guidance, shelter, work, care and even of identity. At a more conscious level, government rules, controls and limits. For western nations, governments are a benevolent force for social progress, with a limited capacity for violence.

The popular idea of government is concentrated in the tag lines of the great republics. The United States of America was founded on unalienable rights, among them Life, Liberty and the pursuit of Happiness, which became the preamble to the declaration of independence. This document was drafted by Thomas Jefferson.

The French Revolution introduced the simpler form, *Liberty, Equality, Fraternity*, also drafted with the help of Jefferson. [30] The alternative was usually *Death*. France also produced the Declaration of the Rights of Man and of the Citizen, now the basis of human rights laws worldwide. The declaration starts with a definition of rights, which are *liberty, property, safety and resistance against oppression*. Olympe de Gouges even produced her own *Declaration of the Rights of Woman and of the Female Citizen*, which had somehow been forgotten in the euphoria of an all-male Revolutionary councils.

Even constitutional monarchies, like the British, are based on some ideals, like the Magna Carta. The British consider that the mother of all parliaments is the cradle of democracy, perhaps forgetting about Athens or Rome.

Democratic processes became ingrained in western European politics as a result of the success of the monastic movement. Their economic power introduced other innovations, such as the rule of written law, due process and trials, but the popular idea of

---

[30] Liberté, égalité, fraternité in the French original. Translation. The concept of liberty, perhaps different to *freedom*, is liberty from feudal oppression, of the sort which existed under the *Ancien Régime*. Equality relates to equal votes, a peculiarly French idea, due to the fact that the nobility and the clergy each held one third of the votes in the French parliaments, when they were held, and the people held the final third. Fraternity introduced the concept of the citizen and the equality of quality.

democracy came from the election of abbots through a fully-franchised vote. [31]

The majority vote became ensconced in parliamentary procedure with the need for approval of the ever-larger tax demands of Edward III, and over the centuries this evolved downwards to the selection of representatives on all sorts of committees.

The Sad Truth

Parliamentary democracy, representative democracy works when the parliament is a collection of the most important tax-payers, negotiating with the tax-collector. Today, parliament is the tax-collector, and its members are tiny contributors, not net contributors at all. This is the starting point for all the problems associated with government, and the cause of misunderstanding between citizens and their leaders.

Government is made up of people and each is an individual. The only people who get to the top of any government organisation are those who are prepared to sacrifice everything to get there. They may not be the brightest, but by the time they get to the top, they have sacrificed their honour, and will then sacrifice anything and everyone else to stay in power, including any principles they had when they started their career. It is

---

[31] Monks managed democracy in their monasteries when they numbered 20 or 40, and were highly successful. However, they restricted democracy to choir monks who had brought property with them when they joined the order, not the lay brothers, serfs, tenants, wives, children or livestock. This was a democracy of shareholders, not residents, employees or customers.

not their choice, it is the nature of the job; they will be destroyed if they tried to hang on to their principles.

Each individual is affected by those around him, his colleagues, his competitors, the media, civil servants, but especially those under him challenging him for his job. Meanwhile, he is calumniating his superiors to get their job.

There are a few saints, but they rarely last long in politics and never reach the top, except to suffer the terrible humiliations of the job. Everybody else in the hierarchy is trying to get something for themselves, for their family, friends, neighbours, employees and, in order to do so, demands money, time or government resources to do so.

Representatives do not represent the wishes and politics of the electorate, not even those who voted for them. Once selected, they behave as they wish. Although at the stump politicians will invoke the will of the People and acknowledge their demands, once in power they will ignore them unless it fits their personal purpose. They have no legal obligation to obey their constituents' demands, and are there to make decisions on their behalf, not to make the decisions that they themselves would have made. Voters delegate the job of governing to politicians, they do not instruct.

The real purpose of government

Popular ideals of democracy, popular government and propaganda have no legal basis. They are not protected in the constitution. Based on law, if the law is corrupt, the government is corrupt. As laws are open to interpretation, the interpretation is open to bribery, politics, personal antagonism, racism, violence and every other ill of society.

British law has long superseded Magna Carta, and the basic rights it contained, the right to work, to pay taxes, the protection of a tax-payers' trade tools, the prohibition on imprisonment, have all disappeared. French human rights were always dependent on the law, and French law now restricts all those rights. Some laws are just as arbitrary and unpopular as the *letter de cachet* that sparked off the Revolution. In 2020, the president rescinded the right to leave home in just such an arbitrary manner.

The US freedoms related only to those British colonials who prepared the paperwork, not to the Indians who surrounded them and occupied the lands they would conquer, or the African slaves who worked their profitable tobacco plantations.

The rights defined by these democratic governments had no legal authority. They were just propaganda, quoted time and time again by politicians buying votes, but ignored the rest of the time. The Magna Carta was regularly quoted by Brexiteers in their campaigns, even while it was already irrelevant. Democracy was eroded. Individuals lost their franchise, through felonies, illegal entry, supporting the losing side in a war, or through simple administrative processes, boundary changes, computer errors, and counting errors. The increase in population, vast increase in taxation and the rise of a public sector that occupies half or more of a nation's economy leaves the third of the population that actually contributes powerless.

Governments in many countries around the world have wiped out 10% of their nation's GDP, killing inward investment, tourism, international travel, airlines, pubs and clubs, restaurant chains, entertainment chains, circuses, sporting franchises, musicians, artists, museums, gyms and leaving many workers in paid employment but with no work to do, including most local civil servants, border force operatives, swimming pool lifeguards, cinema ushers, hairdressers, nail decorators, bus drivers, while many others are unemployed and will remain so for many months to come. It will take years for international travel to recover, and countries like France, Spain, Italy, UK and USA which derive large proportions of their foreign earnings from tourism will suffer large-scale unemployment and economic depression unnecessarily.

However, all is not bad news. The politicians may have destroyed the economy and closed bars and restaurants, but they have kept some of their own facilities open. Both the French and British parliamentarians continue to enjoy the good food and drink and social life of their in-house catering facilities.

In addition, politicians have done nothing to damage their own personal economies. Politicians profit from collecting tax monies and from spending them. COVID will certainly increase government spending, as it already has. Government ministers have rewarded their favourite suppliers with contracts to build track-and-trace systems and Nightingale hospitals, to supply vaccines, masks, gloves and other PPE; they have ordered increased recruitment of police officers and other government agents. All this spending will be rewarded in some way.

Politicians don't have to rely on direct bribes, although these happen in most countries. Indirect bribes are common enough, free lunches, trips and holidays, although these will have to be delayed, internships for children and patronage, book deals and directorships. DSK and Berlusconi were not the only ones enjoying *bunga-bunga* parties, just those who got caught, but the list is as long as the list of politicians.

Equally, tax collection will have to increase. More taxes mean more tax-collectors. Recruitment of agents and establishment of new agencies will require more politicians to manage them all.

History will also require interviews, speeches and books to retell the story of COVID and the brave warriors who saved England in its hour of need.

Politicians are not worried about the outcome of the coronavirus crisis, just how much they can profit from the opportunity.

The frustration felt by the net tax-payers, as well as by many net tax recipients who feel that they don't receive enough, is natural but misplaced. They may blame their government and accuse them of incompetence or stupidity, of cupidity and conspiracy, but in reality there is nothing surprising about the behaviour of government ministers and civil servants.

The problem is that tax-payers and citizens believe government propaganda on the need for government and taxes, just as they believe their own excuses for voting in elections and paying taxes.

The sad truth is that government is merely a hierarchy. Its members have no interest in anything after joining other than climbing it, or at least staying where they are on it. They are not interested in law and order, peace, justice, equality, liberty or fraternity. They may enter government with the repetition of some phrase they have heard, that elicits a positive reaction during recruitment or canvassing, or a positive emotion from their upbringing. However, to rise in a political hierarchy requires ruthless focus on the essential.

Nation state governments operate may be representative democracies, such as that found in the United Kingdom or the United States, others are popular democracies, such as those in China or Vietnam. There remain a few military dictatorships, which rarely last long, reverting to temporary democracies, often with covert military control, such as in Pakistan or Burma. There are a few oligarchies, although more in practice than in legal form. The most common alternative to democracy is absolutism, typical of the Arabian oil states and monarchical kingdoms. Absolute power, backed by legal or constitutional right, is extremely rare, but constitutional monarchies or de facto monarchies are more common, including North Korea and Morocco.

In reality, however, all these governmental systems are similar in the most important aspects. The choice of the leader is, perhaps, different, and that makes a difference to the leader, and maybe in a minor way to the population at large. However, a change in that leader, while shocking for some, is unlikely to make any significant changes to the behaviour of the government or its leaders, to the opposition, to the civil and public servants who make up the vast majority of its employees, or to the children, the unemployed, the prisoners and the sick who make up most of its direct customers.

Governments take considerable trouble, in the case of democracies, at least, to pronounce on the motivation, the preparation and the action that they take on a wide range of issues, from the economy to the climate. These pronouncements are pure propaganda, designed to disguise their behaviour.

Governments as organisations have two behaviours, and their members are responsible as individuals for carrying them out. Individual members, as a result of private interests or the nature of their job in the government, may have additional roles to play.

The first and major role of government is to collect taxes. Governments use many euphemisms for tax, but tax, excise, custom, fines and penalties are common ones. Tax itself is a euphemism for theft. Governments take money with no intention of returning it, no obligation to do so, and provide no service in return.

There is much confusion among happy tax-payers, who claim that in return for paying their taxes they gain certain rights, such as in education, healthcare, unemployment protection, and pensions. This is the first misunderstanding of government. Paying taxes grants no benefits at all. Rights to education and other services administered by government derive from citizenship, age, residence, or additional payment, but never from taxation.

The British constitution is a complex affair, and the role of taxation and services is confused, leading to confusion in scholarly articles and even in Wikipedia pages relating to these subjects. However, this confusion exists only in the English-language versions. In the Spanish-language version of Wikipedia, the role of taxation is spelt out brutally, effectively copying the clear constitution written at the time of the change in government system from military dictatorship to representative democracy under a constitutional monarch. The Spanish constitution clearly states that "tax is a class of tribute …, which is characterized by requiring nothing in return, neither directly nor specifically, on the part of the tax administration." [32] In other words, it is not the payment for a service, not even the contribution for a service. Taxes are the property of the government, and it may do as it pleases with them. Tax-payers have no rights as a result of their contribution.

The second task of government is disbursement, the spending of taxes. Clearly, there is a personal motivation common among all members of the government hierarchies to keep as much of it for themselves, to spend it directly on their own salaries, offices, assistants, expenses, fact-finding trips and as a pension builder for retirement, in preparation for directorships, holidays, and all manner of freebies. There is almost no control on any of this, and only rarely

---

[32] Spanish Wikipedia article on taxation, translated by Google and the Author. The English-language Wikipedia article on taxation starts with the misleading comment "A tax is a compulsory financial charge or some other type of levy imposed on a taxpayer … by a governmental organization *in order to fund government spending and various public expenditures.*" Author's italics. The motivation to collect taxes is to collect taxes. The government propaganda alludes to services rendered, but there are many and better ways to provide services than through government.

does a politician, usually only when in opposition, finds himself convicted of anything worse than fiddling expenses.

Individuals in government do not have time to fight for justice and equality, if they are to keep their job or rise in position. The job of climbing the ladder and staying in power can take up 95% or even 99% of a politician's time. And politicians work long hours if they are to remain in positions of power. However, at some point, real work must impinge on the politicking, and taxes must be raised and spent. At this point, a new set of behaviours appears.

Whereas politicking is a competitive process where everybody is an enemy, taxation is a co-operative process where the other members of the hierarchy are in agreement about everything except the ultimate victim and the primary beneficiary. Each politician and civil servant will have conscious and unconscious reasons for selecting one or other group or individual. This can include bribery and pork barrel politics, but is usually more mundane than anyone can imagine. Part of the infighting will be merely a continuation of the political battles, but here everyone is agreed that tax-payers must be selected, and taxes imposed. At other times, politicians will agree to spend money. Again, the details may cause some political friction whether the money should go to merchant bankers or nurses, but everyone will be in agreement to spend money, because they all benefit as a group. This characteristic of co-operation is at the heart of human society.

The averaging effect of multiple behaviours in very large complex hierarchies with numerous members is that only those behaviours that are innate predominate over time. Any intelligent or technocratic decisions will be cancelled eventually, or simply run over by a tsunami of actions derived genetically, emotionally or by the environment. These are the behaviours that survive.

Homage

The second misunderstanding about government is that taxation is a demand for money with menaces. It is much more than this.

All governments insist on their right to collect taxes, their primary activity. The behaviour of any tax-collector starts with a challenge, usually overt, declaring their authority to demand taxes. It is a seminal moment, and the last opportunity a citizen has before he becomes a tax-payer. A citizen can refuse the challenge, refuse the demand for authority, in accordance with his rights enshrined in the UN Declaration. However, the simplest tax-collector must enforce his authority, and will use extreme violence against anyone refusing him this right.

Taxation starts with this demand for homage. The demand for homage can be a simple request for a signature on a form, or a formal ceremony pledging allegiance to a flag, a nation, a constitution, a monarch, or a religion. Usually, it takes the form of a request to do something, like that of a police officer to switch off an engine, to step out of the car, or to show documents. Submission to the request immediately creates the desired relationship between a government tax-collector and the citizen tax-payer.

A failure to acquiesce, to recognise the authority of the tax-collector to demand homage, leads to rapidly-escalating violence. This violence is inherent in all mammals, and is visible whenever a mammal, especially a male mammal or a female with her cubs is approached by a stranger.

Humans have evolved a strange inhibition, which prevents us from resorting to violence except in specific conditions, when homage is denied or when new taxes are demanded. Adolescents, whose inhibitions are not fully in place when challenged by authority, also react violently to demands for homage, as do drunks, whose inhibitions are removed by alcohol, and old men. [33]

Human inhibition of violence is easily explained through neotenation, the maintenance of a youthful or adolescent state into adulthood. It is a major component of domestication. Like domestication, it involves a loss of freedom, for an ephemeral promise of food, shelter and mating opportunities. A humane death rounds out the offering. As with most ephemeral promises, the reality is somewhat different, but by the time the steak realises that reality, it is too late to mourn the lost mating opportunities.

How, then, does this demand for homage appear in modern society ? The COVID panic has shown that governments worldwide oppress their tax-payers and citizens through lockdowns, distanciation and mask rules. COVID has provided an opportunity for many more people to demand homage. Whereas financial taxes are usually the responsibility of heads of government and their financial ministers, COVID has

---

[33] Co-operation decreases with time spent in any group. On joining, volunteers feel a positive need to contribute, but disillusion is proportional to experience, and by the time they reach maturity they prefer to take rather than put in. [171]

allowed the health branch of government to take control. In many countries and states, they have ordered lockdowns and mask wearing without reference to parliaments or the public, or even to their cabinet colleagues.

The corollary of the desire for homage is that tax-collectors, government leaders, anybody in a hierarchy, but especially those who think that they are at the top of it, hate more than anything else the loss of face from public criticism by those lower than them, especially those that they cannot attack with their forces of law and order. These people include foreigners in foreign countries, financiers from whom they borrow money or receive subsidies, the media, opposition party members benefiting from sovereign immunity, such as parliamentarians, and members of their own political party selection committees.

Often ascribed to Asiatic peoples, loss of face is just as much a European and Anglo-Saxon trait. It may be true that British and American politicians are more used to being insulted. The political system encourages soap-box oratory, TV interviews, and even soul-retching confessions and apologies. However, politicians only do these things if they think it will improve their position in the hierarchy.

Attempts by individuals or groups to refuse new measures, a common problem with demands for taxation, results in a loss of face for the politician, civil servant or police officer implementing them. This loss of face results in the removal of the inhibition against violence, which is unleashed against the refusenik and any bystanders who may have witnessed the embarrassment.

Tax Games

The policies that government ministers prefer to implement are nothing more than a game, designed to show who is boss. Psychological ploys like this one were first analysed scientifically in transactional analysis (TA), and became a specific type of interaction. [34] The key difference between games and other transactions in TA is that there is a payoff, and the interaction is dishonest.

Applying TA to government handling of COVID shows clearly the role of games. A government minister is under pressure from his colleagues and the media, and must make a policy announcement. That decision is likely to enforce some form of confinement and the wearing of masks. Either the citizen acquiesces to the government minister's new edict, or the police beat him up. Refusal by the public to obey the instructions provides a satisfactory excuse should the policy fail or if other ministers criticise or point out more deaths. Meanwhile, the minister challenges the public to catch her out, not wearing a mask, visiting the hair salon, attending a dinner; and when they do, she tells them that she is more important than they are, and has to look good in front of the cameras, communicate clearly and meet other important people. Further questioning results in an angry outburst and more police violence.

Students of TA are familiar with the result. An angry outburst is the proof that the politician is playing

---

[34] Transactional analysis was first described, humorously, by Stephen Potter, but structured in more academic terms by Eric Berne. [169] [170]

a game, an attempt at getting *one-up* on someone else, for the psychological payoff. If the politician was honestly implementing the (intellectually) correct decision and had been caught out cheating, she would have laughed.

COVID-19 is a game that involves many more people than just a government health minister. The game of COVID politics should be described in the terms of transactional analysis to identify the payoff for all the various actors, including those who meekly acquiesce. Those who wear masks or stay at home use their obeisance as a psychological prop to challenge those who don't, either in the street or by ratting on them to the police, or by refusing to serve them in the shops. Check-out assistants find that they have the power of a police officer, and they use it. This behaviour is identical to that of the politicians. The effect of the pecking order in human society is to percolate the need for a psychological payoff down to the lowest orders. At the bottom level, husbands provoke their partners, parents provoke their children, they taunt their pets, trample on their weeds, or simply vandalise inanimate objects.

Brexiteers and MAGA supporters are also playing games. Brexiteers insist that everyone should buy British, while Trump supporters insist on American. They attack those importing foreign cars, raise taxes on imports, while simultaneously demanding better trade deals with those foreign countries. When those foreign countries understandably refuse, Brexiteers and MAGAers blame foreigners for their problems, falling salaries, poor services, poor quality goods. They feel good about themselves, even though their measurable quality of life is reduced.

The act of homage

The demand for homage is an unconscious act. [35] It stems from instinct, a genetically-preprogrammed act which appears automatically under certain circumstances. The perpetrator announces his authority and demands the payment of homage.

The basic principle of homage is that it should be something pointless, painful, embarrassing or costly. Pious behaviour, as homage is called in the faith-based tax domain called religion, is often painful and pointless, and usually costly. Feudal homage is much more about public embarrassment. The expert was Fulk Nerra. When his son, Geoffrey Martel, challenged him, the old master forced the youngster to carry him on his back like a mule.

Any act that is directly and obviously beneficial to the citizen is not an act of homage, it is an investment. Governments rarely advise citizens to invest in pension schemes, and when they do, and these go wrong, they blame the financial advisors who sold them, not the government ministers that promoted them.

Service

---

[35] Most human behaviour is generated unconsciously. Human intelligence is used to justify behaviour, but this process only kicks in after the decision has been made, and often after the action is started, even after the action is completed. Human capacity for self-delusion leads even intelligent beings to believe that they control their behaviour.

Some day, and that day may never come, I'll ask a service of you [36]

The payment of homage rendered, the government agent can progress to the next stage, a request for service. A government agent may do nothing, having received the benefits of the psychological payoff from the demand for homage. However, those people who behave that way will soon succumb to the attacks of their neighbours, who use the established relationship of tax-collector and tax-payer to greater advantage.

Following a demand for homage, the demander needs an army or police force, and for many years they were exactly the same thing, to attack those who refuse to submit. Those who have paid homage, and have a vested interest in the success of their new king, emperor, master, leader, are recruited to provide service in this new venture. While the local resistance is soon crushed, those who are farther away take more resources to crush. Roads may be necessary, and bridges to cross rivers. These demands for service eventually formed into a normal human behaviour called *corvée* labour, which exists across almost all human societies, and all human tax societies.

Service used to involve a weekly stint building roads, repairing bridges or manning the city gates at night. In emergencies, it involved forming a posse to

---

[36] Vito Corleone, after demanding and receiving homage in the form of hand kissing and calling him *Godfather*, from Amerigo Bonasera, the undertaker, who now becomes a *godson* and, therefore, subordinate in the Corleone family, from the eponymous film. [163]

chase after rebels, robbers or escaped prisoners. Ultimately, such service served to defend against incursions by foreign governments, pirates, bandits, and immigrants.

Anybody who could not participate in corvée for any reason, including that he didn't want to, had to pay a *fine*. The fine went towards buying the special equipment that might be necessary, or for paying for professional help. This did not represent a punishment for a criminal act, it was merely part of the arrangement between tax-collector and tax-payer. There were a set of obligations and responsibilities on both parties.

Every citizen had an obligation to provide labour to whoever held authority. The amount varied, and usually increased with time. The fine allowed those whose daily work was profitable to continue working while paying their obligations. As technology increased, the value of unskilled labour decreased and the value of the fine increased.

Government service has grown in complexity, as government revenues have increased and society developed in many different directions. Today, government service can include providing education or healthcare, as well as counting taxes, carrying out military operations abroad, or flying to the moon.

Contribution

At some point, it became more effective to use professional road and bridge engineers, and simply demand citizens that they pay for the costs. Early in the relationship, governments collected money from their citizens. However, there was a better source of money.

Governments who had achieved a desirable relationship with citizens, in which the government demanded and the citizen acquiesced, demanded a share in the citizens' production. It did not matter whether they were miners, farmers, merchants or artisans. The share could be paid in kind, but more and more it is paid in cash.

Taxation, the financial transaction that takes a financial contribution from a producer and gives it to a consumer, reduces money available for investment in the improvement of the production process. Any tax rises, therefore, can reduce future production and future tax revenues.

In ideal situations, the money raised by tax increases is concentrated and then invested in improvement which results in increased production and increased taxes, permitting a reduction in effective rates, and a spiral of imperial growth.

In most cases, however, taxation is squandered on war and luxury, and only a small amount is invested in improvement. This generally leads overall to an improvement in the economy and a subsequent growth in population.

In some cases, taxation is not invested in improvement, and the removal of this money from the economy leads to a spiral of decline, of decreasing production, decreasing tax revenues, and increasing tax rates, in which public anger requires increasing expenditure on law and order. Imperial decline in these conditions is exceptionally difficult to prevent.

Funding

Service and contribution are necessary to fund the government. Government members need to cover their own costs and pay for their luxury lifestyle. They need to offer patronage and reward those who pay them homage, otherwise they will calumniate them.

Unfortunately, government members are not good at managing budgets, and they typically overspend. As a result, they are always looking for ways to increase service and contribution.

Every complaint or request by citizens are opportunities to increase taxes. Whether they will be used, depends on who makes the real decisions.

The typical organisation deciding on who to tax and how much to demand is a parliament. The original idea of a parliament, like that of England and then Britain, was to assemble the most important tax-payers of the country and agree to their contribution for the next year. They could agree that, in exchange for certain rights, exemptions and monopolies, they would contribute the customary taxes and any special taxes.

Most countries that experience long-term growth are managed in this way. The British parliament of the imperial years was made up mostly of the major tax-payers of the country. The English Great Council was made up of the lords and bishops who not only paid the most taxes but also controlled the economy. The United States was initially set up by the largest tax-payers of the 13 Colonies, George Washington and Thomas Jefferson.

Parliaments organised in this way rarely voted to increase taxes, except when their economic investments were threatened. There was no incentive to pay more in expenses or administrators' salaries

Modern parliament, however, is the tax-collector, the equivalent of a king, while the tax-payer is now excluded except for a single vote every four or five years. It is no longer a suitable organism for collaborative negotiation. Net tax-payers in Britain, for example, no longer include the richest men, the monarchy, the aristocracy, the top businessmen, and the media barons. All of these are either net tax recipients or not resident for tax purposes. Through trusts, offshore investments, offshore tax-residency, the operation of limited liability corporations or of tax-free charities, the richest and most powerful in the land may belong to the House of Lords or Commons without paying more in tax than they receive in benefits.

As governments get bigger, in other words, as the tax take increases, and especially as it passes 50% of the territory economy, 50% of the population is also directly or indirectly dependent on the government. As these are also voters, they will vote for whichever party promises to increase their handouts the most, in other words, which promises to increases taxes the most.

As the tax system is controlled by holders of a monopoly of violence, it allows the tax-collector to increase tax rates without worrying about the consequences. The result is that, at some point, more tax-payers work for the tax-collector than for themselves, and the economy spirals into terminal decline. This has been the history of every tax territory, from that of Ur of the Chaldees to the British Empire.

Collapse is affected despite the efforts of any intelligent opposition. While taxes are low, there is much debate between different parties about the best means of raising them and spending them. When taxes are high, however, there may be much debate, but there is little difference in execution. Almost no modern political party removes taxes or expenditures already in place, regardless of how much they criticised them before coming to power.

One solution would be to focus government action on improving the economy. However, this abstract euphemism hides some brutal truths. Improvements in an economy can only come from a limited number of initiatives, including increased expenditure on communications improvements, and reduced taxation. Neither of these suggestions will find favour in a difficult economy. The remaining options are increased unemployment, the lower wages that allows, from increased exploitation of natural resources, alive, dead and never alive, with its attendant pollution, and with increases in population, usually through increased immigration, with its inevitable increase in population density, housing prices, local services, food, greater inequality. Decreases in population may lead to temporary, superficial improvements, by removing scroungers, hobos, the homeless, and illegal immigrants, but as the problem is not them, it will have no more benefit than the tiny reduction in their social security payments.

The opportunities for waste are endless. Taxes spent on improving productive assets are usually a tiny fraction of total taxes extracted from the economy. The rest is squandered buying votes and on luxury. The protection of non-productive or non-reproductive members of society is economic suicide. Although it is popular with self-declared socialists and many liberals, it is the cruellest form of slavery. Equally, the taxation, persecution, execution or ostracism of the wealthy and successful is an even faster form of economic suicide.

There is no magic money, regardless of what social economists and idealists might claim. A simple experiment is all that is needed to prove that claim wrong. Anyone can print money, there is no need to be a bank or a government. Anybody with desktop publishing software on a computer can design a banknote and anybody with a colour printer can print the banknotes. Will anyone accept them ? Not without collateral. No serious businessman or woman will accept what amounts to an IOU without protection.

Governments are in the same situation. They can print more money, but if they do not have collateral, no-one will accept it. Printing money is a good way of reducing the attractiveness of government collateral.

It sounds good, to tax the rich and give to the poor, like Robin Hood. The demonization of bankers, lenders, Jews, millionaires, billionaires, bishops, abbots, aristocrats and kings is just as effective and just as incorrect as the demonization of any other minority or vulnerable group.

The other problem is that politicians always want to sound positive. They claim that they want to have a strong economy, lots of jobs, low unemployment, and high wages. These things are not possible together. A strong economy needs low wages and high unemployment. It is not possible long term to manage high growth and low unemployment, except possibly with a large transient workforce and large-scale immigration.

Bankers, governments, politicians and the rich generally want to avoid negative interest rates or high inflation. They are happy to have high interest rates. It is only competition between bankers that reduces interest rates. Meanwhile poor people and borrowers are happy to have low or negative interest rates and low inflation.

As a result, governments and their central reserve banks carry out illogical and often disastrous policies to protect the wealth of the rich. Governments are the largest borrowers in the world, so they insist on low interest rates. Those with money to invest prefer to spend it on land, charities, or works of art, rather than government bonds, industrial plant or transport infrastructure.

Fortunately, governments are more interested in protecting the wealth of the rich than they are in reducing the government debt. This is because the members of government see a life beyond politics. The massive debt of the United States and the United Kingdom would be best managed by a prolonged period of high inflation. Inflation would wipe out the savings of the middle-classes, the retired pensioners living in their own homes and the super-rich, but it would also reduce the real value of the government's debt. This is an unlikely scenario, as in modern finance governments can constantly increase their debt. [37]

---

[37] The US debt amounts to $23 Trillion at the time of writing in 2020.

Government policies

Regardless of political party, most governments follow the same policies as their predecessors. 99% or more of the legal system remains the same, 99% of the civil servants remain the same. Over 4 or 5 years, some new laws are introduced, but little enough to change anything important.

Few real changes exist in political history. Stalin's move to industrialise the Soviet Union after the death of Lenin, which permitted his survival under the German onslaught of Barbarossa; the execution or exile of the French aristocracy, landlords and farmers-general at the start of the French Revolution; the eviction of the Jews from Germany after 1933, or the Huguenots from France after St Bartholomew; the flight of the communists from Spain in 1938-9; these were major changes, but the victory of a conservative prime minister in an election presages no greater change than the colour of a tie.

British governments nationalised industries during the 1950s and 1960s and denationalised them during the 1980s and 1990s. But the same factories produced the same cars, the same hospitals carried out the same operations. The same miners, managers and doctors carried on with their jobs.

Revolutionary changes, improvements, even, that do happen are eventually eradicated, or converted into a system of oppression. The greatest force for good is the right to education, especially a free education, as provided by schools, libraries, encyclopaedias, and the internet. Education used to be the privilege of the rich because knowledge itself was expensive to collect and diffuse. The Enlightenment and the global media have proliferated this knowledge, but it was the attitude of the Enlightened that led to demands for public, free education.

Public free education became a right at the same time as it became an obligation. Instead of granting the public a benefit, it increased taxation by providing a controlling mechanism which feeds government propaganda, trains children in its language and processes, and therefore supplies its future administrators, soldiers and tax-payers.

There was for a short time the ideal of free healthcare for everyone, but this lasted only as long as it took to realise that there was no money to do so. Britain, one of the first countries to introduce a nationalised health service, had had free healthcare for generations of the working class, while the middle classes and aristocracy paid, usually through the system of private rooms. The new NHS soon introduced charges, for glasses, for prescriptions, for private rooms, for dental work,

A similar situation resulted from demands for social insurance, protection against unemployment. Such a protection now exists only with an obligation to work.

As for governments' oft-claimed benevolence and care for the public, no government has lasted after banning tobacco, alcohol, or war, and none so far has dared to ban sugar. Successful bans on certain classes of weapons have been limited to those least useful, and have usually been circumvented. Biological and chemical weapons are notoriously unreliable, and their current use is reserved against tax-payers and citizens rather than foreign enemies who do not have the equipment to protect themselves. The useful ban on mines ignores the much greater problem of unexploded artillery ordnance and the legal fiction of cluster bombs, which are merely air-dropped mines. [38]

Attempts to ban nuclear weapons failed at the start, as the first country to develop them used them. Since then, that country has tried to prevent their proliferation with the promise that it will give up its own nuclear arsenal. [39] Like all ephemeral promises, its repetition hides a deliberate proliferation in delivery mechanisms and warheads, enough to obliterate the

---

[38] The 1997 Ottawa Treaty banned the use of mines, but it took the Oslo convention of 2008 to ban the use of submunition cluster bombs for mine dispersal. The United States of America has not signed the later convention. Britain has signed and ratified the treaty, but its cluster bombs are still killing civilians in countries like Yemen, attacked by Saudi Arabia, which is equipped with British aircraft and weapons.

[39] The nuclear powers, USA, UK, France, Russia and China have pursued nuclear disarmament for fifty years, and are further away today than they were when they started. Their behaviour has merely confirmed the need to possess nuclear weapons in order to achieve sovereign status. Both the US and Russia have significantly reduced the number of warheads in their arsenals, but have delivery systems that are almost entirely based on intercontinental missiles or stealth bombers with a much higher potential success rate. France and China have significantly increased their nuclear arsenals since signing the treaty, while Britain has reduced its numbers while improving their capability. Meanwhile, India, Pakistan, Israel and North Korea have developed their military nuclear capability. None of the current nuclear powers has plans to discontinue their possession, France, UK and USA are currently designing their next generation nuclear ballistic missile submarines for operation until 2070 (UK) and 2080 (US).

civilian population of any other country, of a dozen other countries. [40]

The real history of the last 75 years – not an idyllic democracy, but ever encroaching totalitarianism

First they came for the socialists, and I did not speak out

Human behaviour is a constant, at least over a period as long as a generation. There is nothing new about the behaviour of national leaders, members of government, advisors, voters, tax-payers and the unemployed in 2020, and that of their equivalents in

---

[40] To be fair to governments, other organisations are equally incompetent. The Nobel organisation awards an annual peace prize, but some of its recipients are war mongers. Theodore Roosevelt had barely pocketed his cheque when he ordered the invasion of Cuba, followed by the conquest of the Panama canal zone; Woodrow Wilson created the conditions for today's conflict in the Middle East; Cordell Hull obstructed the emigration of Jews from Nazi Germany and occupied Europe to the United States. Hull was not anti-semitic, although touchy about his ancestry; he married a Jew. Henry Kissinger and Lê Đức Thọ shared the prize in 1973, ostensibly for agreeing to end the Vietnam War; Kissinger was awarded it while carrying out a secret bombing of Cambodia and supporting the military coup in Chile, while Lê Đức Thọ refused his award and within a year was marching on Saigon. Aung San Suu Kyi's non-violent struggle for democracy and human rights lasted only as long as it took her to come to power in Myanmar, when she directed her country's military forces to use violence against minority groups who insisted on their human rights. At least, they refused to award any prizes during the world wars, except to the Red Cross,

1920, or 1820, or 1720. However, for those who led a sheltered life, it may have appeared that during their childhood, or during their parents' era, things were better, more just and more equitable, than they are today.

For 75 years after the Second World War, Europe has lived an almost ideal lifestyle. Most white, middle class adults have benefited from a liberty to study, work, travel, spend and associate without government interference. Taxation has been almost invisible. The acquiescence to tax-raising rights, a minimal payment of homage to an ideal, constitution, flag or anthem, some civic classes at school, has created an image of freedom that most of our ancestors could never imagine.

Military service has all but disappeared except for those who volunteer as professionals. The arrival of armies or militias, commandeering transport, labour and accommodation, and stealing or buying at privileged rates or with IOUs consumables, raw materials, tools, livestock is a thing of the past. Police checkpoints with armed guards demanding identity papers, travel permits, justifications are just horrible memories now turned into drama or comedy for the cinema or television. Empty shops, queues for food and the non-availability of essential medicines, were the preserve of anti-communist propaganda.

Much of that freedom translated to a relative freedom to behave in the same way abroad, in almost any country in the world. The collapse of the Iron Curtain left only Saudi Arabia and North Korea as difficult destinations, and only the war-torn American colonies of Iraq and Afghanistan as too dangerous. A few of the Andaman Islands remain the only non-nation populated territories that are impossible to visit.

However, this ideal portrait hides a sordid truth. Although for the vast majority of the middle-class population of western nations this is an accurate picture, for many others it is not. Only the very young, the unintelligent and the uneducated are surprised by government corruption and police brutality, by massive unemployment, declining living standards, increased pollution. Protestors tend to be a combination of all three. Anyone with a long memory, critical observation skills and impartiality can list similar events from their own country going back centuries.

The catalogue of disastrous human behaviour which could otherwise be catalogued as incompetent, evil or selfish is the popular history of the world. Every country, nationality, religion has their story. The repetition, at generation gaps, is here offered just as an example of the last hundred years for a few countries. There is here, and everywhere else, no sign that intelligence works for the greater good, the improved demography or economy. Rather, human agency is accidental, often cruel and pointless, rarely comic, but always clearly aimed at enforcing homage first, then service and finally a financial contribution to pay for the disaster.

This chapter is simply to show disbelievers that in any country governments and their agents behave violently, arbitrarily and with no thought of justice, fairness, equality, liberty or fraternity. All these stories of brutality and incompetence can be seen as intelligent and, given the almost total immunity of government agents in general, the victims could be considered lucky.

Many societies have witnessed mass torture and extermination, in the last 100 years of intelligent human evolution.

However, attempts to ascribe specific behaviour to either intelligence or incompetence fail inevitably on detail definition. Only from the point of view of a specific actor and with a specific objective in mind does it permit to make an act intelligent or incompetent. At no time does intelligent design enter the picture. Usually, the actors are those who suffer the most. Police brutality rarely improves a police officer's career prospects, his health or his wealth.

The only viable explanation is that police behaviour, and that of their victim, follows genetically predetermined paths. The police officer, often stressed by the need to confront fit, strong, aggressive young men and women, would like as a minimum a level of respect. Police officers may not be experts on the law, although many barrack-room lawyers imagine that they are, nor are they always sure about their rights as officers, but at no time will they be willing to hear criticism of their imagined position of authority. In any case, most police officers behave in a pure tax-collector way, demanding homage immediately by asking the victim to do something pointless, like switching off the car engine or the radio, letting them into the

The only acceptable response is acquiescence. Any other response will result in an increase in the level of aggression. The usual level of aggression is that normally found in encounters between strange mammals. Death is not necessarily the objective of mammal-mammal encounters, just a successful defence of territory or property, including mating rights. Death is far more common as a direct result of human confrontations due to the propensity for using tools and weapons. Few animals use sticks and stones, and none fashion them specifically to hurt, maim or kill, yet there is ample evidence that humans have done just that for thousands of years. The rise and fall in human death portrayed by historians is not an indication of increased violence, merely the effectiveness of weapons and of modern medicine.

United Kingdom

The history of British government and policing is one of benevolent and reasonable policies. Britain was unusual as a country in that most of its armed forces were abroad after the disastrous experience of the New Model Army, a highly-professional body of disciplined competent men who decided that they should run the country. British politicians never made the same mistake again, and have since maintained as few military forces as possible in Britain, and those they did have they divided up into three to minimise the chances that any of them could ever take power again. As a result, Britain always had few forces to deal with large-scale insurrection, and even fewer after the last revolt in Scotland in 1745.

A hundred years after the '45, however, millions of Scottish and Irish immigrants were the cause of some consternation for the middle class of London. The drunkenness, promiscuity, wholesale theft and begging which extended into the richer quarters and suburbia led to demands for protection, containment and eradication of the scourge of poverty and crime.

The police force introduced in Britain by Robert Peel set out to protect the middle classes from the working classes and the unemployed who threatened to engulf them. Peel adopted a utilitarian and benevolent attitude more usual in medical circles than law enforcement; first, do no evil. He refused to arm the new police, and therefore protected them to some extent by granting them immunity.

The British bobby used to be a byword for community policing. The truth is that for a hundred years after the Peelers were invented, they were. Unarmed, selected for their height at a time when English were badly nourished, educated but working class, the image of PC Plod was that of a stalwart defender of middle and upper-class England from the intrusions of the low life that infested the docks and industrial zones of Britain.

It was almost unheard of for British police to kill anyone. PC George Cooke was hanged for the murder of Maud Smith, in 1893, beating her head in with his truncheon in what appeared to have been a personal quarrel.

British policing began to change in the 1940s, thanks to censorship, wartime propaganda and the Cage. German prisoners suffered psychological interrogation at the Cage, in west London. Instead of torture and deprivation, they were housed in communal areas, where intelligence officers listened in to their private conversations.

Towards the end of the war, however, with ULTRA providing all the intelligence the British needed, the Cage became only a cage, and those inside increasingly came from the SS, whose atrocities were now common knowledge thanks to the BBC and the British propaganda units. Those police officers manning the cage, left to their own devices, took it upon themselves to teach the Jerries a lesson, and they did.

This muscular approach to policing carried on after the war, both in metropolitan policing and in colonial affairs, in Malaya and Kenya, Hong Kong and wherever it was needed. Returning home, they found the crowded streets of Britain's inner cities populated by the same African, Asian and Caribbean populations they had despisingly oppressed abroad.

It didn't help that some of these immigrants turned to crime, or that those without sufficient work stalked the streets at night looking for action, women or just to pass the time. Surprisingly for a colonising country, the British were often surprised to see colonial immigrants wandering the streets at night, as if they had somehow been used to staying in at night in their mansions back home. Even today, much of Asian and African life is led in the street, outdoors, where the weather is suitable and the innate gregariousness seeks solace in the company of anyone similarly afflicted.

The police idyll lasted until the 1960s. When terrorists and bank robbers started using guns, the police retaliated with their own weapons. This led to an increase in muscular policing, and the shoot-to-kill policy introduced by Margaret Thatcher to deal with IRA terrorists (but not to deal with the Protestant ones). This liberty to kill continues to this day, successfully killing retired cabinet-makers with a plastic bag containing a wooden chair leg, a Brazilian tourist, as well as disarmed terrorists and the odd bank robber.

Police brutality is not limited to shooting innocent people. They also beat them to death. Blair Peach was only the most famous victim of the notorious SPG. Britain's riot police was forced to close down after too many, too public cases of brutality; it was replaced by the much bigger, but more secretive TSG, who garnered their own bad publicity by killing Ian Tomlinson.

Police mistook Stephen Waldorf for an attempted murderer and shot him four times, then another five times, and again twice more. Such police brutality might have been excused, as even though Stephen Waldorf was innocent, the police were under the stress of searching for a man who had already tried to kill a fellow officer, and had fired at security guards and other police officers and was known to be armed and dangerous. Such sympathy that the police who shot Stephen Waldorf might have garnered would have been lost as, once collapsed on the bonnet of the car, helpless, obviously unarmed, and clearly not the right person, the police officer whose job was to identify him pointed his gun between Waldorf's eyes, said "OK, cocksucker" and pulled the trigger. Only his empty revolver saved Waldorf's life for the pistol whipping he now received, witnessed by his distraught companions and several onlookers. The judge trying the police officers charged with attempted murder ordered the jury to find them not guilty, while the miscreant whose mistaken identity had caused all this trouble for Stephen Waldorf was found guilty of attempted murder and sentenced to life imprisonment.

The European Court of Human Rights has challenged the British police on their behaviour in relation to the Azelle Rodney killing. They state that intervening with a known criminal, who may be armed and dangerous, with an armed response unit, is tantamount to a death warrant. Any sudden movement by the suspect, which is perfectly reasonable when surprised by a rush of armed men, who are often in civilian clothes. Police were lucky for their case that Azelle Rodney turned out to be in a car loaded with guns and had a house full of stash, but their errors are too great and the uncontrolled ferocity of firing multiple rounds (when a trained assassin would use no more than 2) shows that this is a lustful joy killing.

John Charles de Menezes was killed by such a bloodthirsty police officer, and the majority of the deaths on Bloody Sunday were killed by a single soldier with the same lust for death. The failure of the police and Army to deal with these individual cases refutes any suggestion that police forces are staffed mostly by good officers with only the odd bad apple. In the case of de Menezes the police officer is a "serial killer", nicknamed thus by the current head of the Metropolitan Police, who was sued successfully for the comment. Not only did the individuals responsible for these murders avoid serious censure, but their colleagues and superiors failed to prevent the murders, failed to protect the victims, failed to arrest the perpetrators, and failed to prosecute them. The failure reaches the top of the legal system, and includes the public, the media and the jury as well as coroners, judges, ministers and prime ministers.

Britain's behaviour outside the narrow confines of South-East England, however, leaves much to be desired. England's brutal conquests of Wales, Scotland

and Ireland are well known. After the conquests and the initial insurrections, there was little trouble in Wales and Scotland, but Ireland saw regular violence.

The worst cases of government violence occurred in Ireland during the war for self-determination and independence, and along the border after Irish Independence and before the Irish civil war, when the Black and Tans and the B-Specials were a byword for extra-legal murder, arson and violence. Trouble flared up again in Ulster in the 1950s and again in the 1960s as Britain refused to recognise the civil rights of its minorities. Violence remained at a high level and was even exported to Europe, funded by the United States of America and equipped by Americans, Czechs and Libyans on the one side, and funded by crime and armed by the British government on the other. The killings continued in Ireland until the Good Friday Agreement in 1998, leaving a tally of 3,532 dead. Over a thousand were British soldiers, reservists, prison and police officers, but almost two thousand were just civilians caught up in the crossfire. Of these, 25 were shot by the police, including three members of the British army in mufti. The police also beat 2 more to death, while the army shot 14 on Bloody Sunday. [41]

It is disconcerting that there have been Bloody Sundays in 1887, 1911, 1920, 1921 and 1972, in which the British forces of law and order attacked the citizens they exist to protect. Four thousand police charged an Irish and Fabian march in Trafalgar Square, and wounded 75 seriously, but only one died of his wounds

---

[41] Additional Northern Irish citizens were killed by police and soldiers in operations mounted by civilians. [142]

in the 1887 version. In 1911, Liverpool police charged strikers, wounding 350, while soldiers opened fire on unruly natives a few days later, killing two. During the Irish war for independence, British forces opened fire at a Dublin sports event, killing 14. In 1921, Belfast Protestants and police opened fire indiscriminately at catholic houses and citizens, killing 17 on the Bloody Sunday itself, and another 11 dead or dying of their wounds in the week that followed. While never on the scale of the Amritsar massacre, these killings were well documented and published immediately in Britain and abroad. The killing of women and children, often named and even photographed, had a much more powerful effect than that of nameless Sikhs, or, rather, than that of Sikhs all of whom had one of the same two names. [42]

In addition to openly-approved murders, there were a number of murders committed by the Protestant paramilitaries that are thought to have been ordered or recommended by the British police, through the activities of their informant, Brian Nelson, who arranged such things. This included the murder of lawyer Pat Finucane in 1989. Such an informer may have influenced the perpetrators of the Loughinisland massacre, in which 6 Catholics were killed while watching a football match. The murderers possibly included a British soldier and an informer.

As well as murdering its own citizens, the British government imprisoned them concentration

---

[42] Additional Bloody Sundays exist in the history of the USA, Russia, Germany, Italy, Nova Scotia, Alsace, Germany (again), Poland (three times), the US again, Turkey and Lithuania.

camps. They used such camps in South Africa after the Boer War to house millions of Boer women and children, 26,000 of whom died. In Northern Ireland, they built the H-Blocks of the Maze Prison, where British citizens suffered long incarceration without cause or trial.

When it couldn't use emergency powers, as it did in the colonies and Northern Ireland, the police turned to the traditional tactics. Fitting up the Birmingham 6, the Guildford 4 and the Maguire 7. Even if some of the convicted had had some involvement in the crimes, their conviction effectively ended the investigation and would have prevented a subsequent prosecution. For the Guildford bombing, the IRA had even announced publicly that the convicted were innocent.

France

Alors, nous ne sommes pas dans le même camp [43]

France has a long history of firing on its own people, at least since Napoleon Bonaparte took control

---

[43] "Well, we are not on the same side." Didier Lallement, Paris Prefect of Police, a political but uniformed role, commenting to a protestor during the Yellow Vest marches in 2019. His Freudian slip is a perfect example of the difference between "to protect and to serve", the euphemistic description of the police role, as understood by most innocent children, and the brutal reality. France, like every other democracy and dictatorship, is a police state. The police service does not exist to protect the population, from each other or from the state itself, but to protect the state from its citizens, tax-payers and critics at home and abroad.

of the country with a "whiff of grapeshot". [44] French governments have little reticence when it comes to ordering their police into action, and no shame afterwards. [45]

Long before Adolf Hitler's German forces demanded the removal of the French Jews, the free Vichy leaders imposed their own anti-Semitic laws, and

---

[44] Thomas Carlyle's description of the ending of the popular French Revolution, and the beginning of Bonapartist military absolutism, on 13 Vendémiaire, Year 4.

[45] The author's own experience of suffering a beating by the CRS, the French riot police, on New Year's Eve 2002/2003 under the Eiffel Tower, was more comic than painful, but gives a good indication that charging riot police can appear anywhere, at any time, and without any justification. The old man who fell over while running away, and ended up on his back with his arms and legs flailing while he was unnecessarily gassed in the face with pepper spray, found it less comic. The riot police themselves probably suffered. They feared for their lives, hence the charge. But they feared for their lives because they had ordered a hundred thousand people to disperse, and felt frustrated that they were not immediately obeyed. Instead, bottles started flying in. For riot police to deploy in Paris, with a million people from all over Europe visiting to celebrate the New Year, is absurd. However, a hundred thousand police officers are on duty every year, in a vain attempt to prevent the thousands of burnt cars offered up every year to St Sylvester, including usually a couple of hundred police cars. Burning police cars and stations is a French rite of passage, and hardly a night goes past when one or other does not erupt in flames. *Banlieu* police stations face regular attacks, usually by friends or neighbours of arrested delinquents. Ten in the first ten months of 2020 in the author's *département*. The attackers currently deploy powerful but illegal fireworks, stones, iron bars and the odd Molotov cocktail. Usually, the police respond with rioter-friendly sting-ball grenades rather than firearms or batons. The level of stress felt by police in these circumstances can only be partially imagined.

incarcerated 40,000 foreign Jews in concentration camps, with hundreds dying in the winter of 1941. [46] This programme was defended by its French organisers as similar to British and American incarceration of aliens, partly as a protection against a possible fifth column in the event of invasion, and partly a sop to the popular xenophobia encouraged by years of nationalism and the success of international communism.

The Vichy police also incarcerated their own left-wing politicians.

In Occupied France, the French police obliged the Jewish population to register, to announce themselves if trading, and to wear the start of David on their clothing. The police controlled those who refused, as they might today control those who refuse to wear masks.

Meanwhile, and even while Germany and the Soviet Union were allied by the Molotov-Ribbentrop pact, the police in the Occupied zone arrested the leadership and many of the rank and file of the communist party, including those who had fought in Spain in the International Brigades. These were sent to concentration camps in Algeria.

In order to understand how the French population reacted to the increasing *collaboration* - the word which would define the worst crime of the Second World War was actually the official Vichy government programme of *rapprochement* to the German Nazi policies – the French police set about spying on the post and telephone service.

------

[46] [152]

To help control the French population better, the Vichy government created the national police service, the *Police Nationale*, nationalising the municipal police forces and weeding out the many anti-Nazis in the process. Their uniform today still boasts the *fasces*, international symbol of fascism.

The invasion of the Soviet Union in 1941 led in France to open war between the remaining communists and the German forces, and the French police retaliated by arresting five thousand. The assassination of German officers led to the retaliatory execution of multiple prisoners; although the executions were carried out by Germans, the arrests and handover were by French police. The French went on to arrest thousands of mainly communist resistants, torturing and executing those most troublesome, including the readership of *L'Humanité*, the international socialist newspaper. It took two *Brigades spéciales* to destroy the Communist resistants and put an end to the assassinations and bombings.

The war against Russia also increased the epressure eon Jews throughout the occupied countries nof Europe, and din France, the French police arrested and deported 40,000 in 1942, foreigners and French alike.

The initial success of the Anglo-American alliance and its operation *Torch* in 1942 caused more misery for the mainland French at the hands of their police force. It took 9,000 police officers and gendarmes to evacuate the 27,000 inhabitants of the Old Port of Marseilles, carrying only hand luggage, before its destruction by the German armed forces. The French police deported two thousand to extermination camps.

German failures in the East also led to demands throughout western Europe for recruits for labour. In France, conscription had been ended in 1940, with the imprisonment of the French conscription army after the Armistice. Now, a two year obligation to serve as labour was reintroduced, covering the three years of recruits available.

Many of these potential recruits decided to evade the obligatory labour service and fled to the *maquis*, where they would form the new, post-communist, resistance, now aided by America and Britain.

Many of the new maquisards were themselves children of police officers, and the behaviour of the Germans, the occupation of the *Zone libre* after the fall of the French possessions in North Africa and the realisation that Allied victory was inevitable, led many police officers to resign, actively help the resistance or passively obstruct, or fail in, their service. Vichy reacted by the creation of fascist militias, specifically to fight the resistance forces.

The French police saved themselves as a group from the humiliations that came after Liberation by starting that movement themselves in Paris. A sixth of the nine hundred liberationists killed in the 6 days of fighting were police officers. De Gaulle's new chief of police gave the usual politician's speech of welcome, admiring their service to France, their honour, their loyalty etc. [47] They immediately set out to reinforce this view by rounding up collaborators, and making them

---

[47] De Gaulle and all his Free French forces had been tried and condemned *in absentia* by the legal French courts as traitors.

available to the kangaroo courts set up to try them. Even so, ten thousand of their number suffered trial, punishment or sacking. [48]

The police that operated after liberation were little better than those who had operated before, and wer often the same people. Hundreds of militiamen were brutally beaten, tortured and killed in the weeks after liberation, some by individuals seeking revenge, others by groups seeking to assuage their lust for violence, still others by organised forces of the Free French. A few were granted the dubious pleasure of a kangaroo court to sanction their death, as at Le Grand Bonnard, where 76 miliciens were shot and buried in unhallowed ground.

The introduction of ex-post facto laws, illegal under the Declaration of Human Rights, permitted the prosecution of civil and police leaders. A hundred thousand were convicted and punished with national degradation, a particularly republican punishment which involved a form of internal professional ostracism.

The Free French forces carrying out the *épuration*, the cleansing, were just as guilty as the population at large. The simplest cases involved the women guilty of collaborating intimately with Germans; they suffered the humiliation of a head shave, a naked streak through their village being kicked and beaten by their neighbours, and the ostracism from their community. Their 200,000 children suffered the insults

---

[48] [153]

and slurs of their neighbours with collaborator and resistant parents. [49]

The leaders of the Vichy government and its police organisations, including the Milice, were executed or imprisoned. Another 8,775 collaborators were executed, illegally, with no attempt to apprehend or reprehend the *malfaiteurs*. 97,000 were condemnded by courts, including by courts set up to try people who had committed no crime, except to collaborate with the civic authorities of the time. Fifteen hundred were legally executed.

It is tempting to blame the actions of the French police during occupation on their German invaders, the failure of the French governments of appeasement, and on the complications of life in an impossible situation. Had Germany survived as an independent country, and de Gaulle never become leader of France, then perhaps the resulting *épuration* and the condemnation and execution of the collaborators would never have happened.

However, there is no evidence that anything in France has changed since the fall of fascism, the occupation of France by Gaullist forces, or the installation of a new political corps.

The most recent problems of civil obedience caused by COVID-19 and protests against the illogical and dangerous *confinement*, the obligation to wear masks and the requirement to sign an affidavit for every one of the limited rights of excursion merely joined those already ongoing as part of the yellow vest protests against increased taxes, especially on diesel fuel which

---

[49] [154]

hit the sole trader and self-employed community particularly hard.

Interior minister Gérald Darmanin spoke to the press, saying "Je n'abandonnerai pas les policiers" but leaving no doubt that he has already abandoned the electorate and the public. The sad truth is that a minister is no more than the figurehead boss of his ministry. He has no real power other than what he is allowed to exercise by the real powers in the hierarchy. His power extends only to the voice he uses reading prepared speeches and agreed soundbites on interviews.

Police action in France is generally robust, led by Didier Lallement, brought in after politicians' favourite restaurant, *Fouquets* on Champs-Élysées was burned to the ground by the yellow jackets. His job was to take control of Paris' streets, but all he has achieved is a series of running brutal battles with the public, the press and the politicians themselves, who have found themselves, if they are not at the highest levels of the hierarchy, and even when they are wearing their badges of office, shut off from their own constituents, offices and events.

The latest and most grotesque *affaire* is the *loi de sécurité globale* designed to offer not global security, but protection to police officers from the publicity of the press and protestors. [50] Criminalising the distribution

---

[50] As usual, the defence and the criticism of this law by those who should know better are neither intelligent nor practical. The criticisms misrepresent the law while ignoring the total failure of the legal system to protect the public from the police, and its defenders ignore its pointlessness and its one sided nature. The law itself covers many issues, a typical political gambit to obscure the most offensive. The article relating to images of police officers

by social media of police officers' personal data, including name and behaviour, merely adds to enormous immunity already possessed by any government agent in France, protected against any *outrage* by a stack of laws and a prosecution system guaranteed to convict.

France is no difference than any other country, its leaders are protected by sovereign immunity and the forces of law and order are usually protected by the same *de jure* rights as well as by *de facto* immunity. The

---

merely renders illegal the publishing of any personal data such as images taken during official operations with the intention of damaging their physical or moral integrity. There is no restriction on the freedom of the press to provide to the proper authorities such information as they may collect with a view to the prosecution of crimes committed by police officers. This article is unnecessary as such behaviour as conspiracy or encouraging attacks on police officers is already a crime of attacking the authority of the police. The police certainly need no additional protection. If this article protected equally the rights of individual members of the public, it might still be pointless, as French individual rights are strongly protected by laws. The real problem is never when one individual appears against another individual in a court of law, but when an individual is up against a member of the police. This law, which does nothing to upset the powers of the press, protects the guilty police officer from trial by social media. It is sad that such methods are today the only ones capable of resulting in exoneration for an innocent (or innocent of some of the charges) victim, or of prosecution of a guilty police officer. It is rare for a police officer to suffer a conviction for actions carried out in uniform, much less to go to jail or to spend any considerable amount of time in prison. Article 24 makes it even less likely, but not for the reasons claimed. The real problems are trial by media and the total failure by every legal system in the world, from the police officers themselves to the juries and voters and tax-payers who support them, to provide adequate checks and balances.

laws that prohibit treason, high treason, the very French *lèse-majesté* are archaic but their modern versions are effective enough. In any case, most members of the higher echelons of government are much more interested in seeing their critics savagely beaten or even shot than in seeing them in court where they will have the chance to repeat their probably accurate and humorous insults.

Protests of 2020 are merely the latest in an endless series of protests and police beatings. In 2007, Paris' poorest suburbs of Sarcelles and Gonesse literally burned following the death in Villiers-le-Bel of two motorcyclists, crushed under a police car. Both the riders and the police officer driving the car were breaking the French highway code at the time of the accident. Fearing a lynching, the police officers abandoned the scene of the accident, a crime, as did the ambulance drivers and paramedics who arrived later, also a crime. Two weeks of rioting ensued. A hundred police officers were injured, eighty by buckshot and five by heavier calibre weapons. The police driver eventually received a 6-month suspended sentence for killing two young men. The rioters, meanwhile, went to jail for up to 15 years for wounding police officers.

Didier Lallement is only the latest prefect of police accused of brutality. For many years, Paris was ruled by Maurice Papon, whose name was a byword for police brutality. In 1962, his troops attacked a peaceful march of socialist and communist strikers from the CGT, trapping some in an underground station entrance and killing 9 of them with metal street furniture that they ripped up to throw down on them. [51]

Four months earlier, Prefect Papon had ordered his police to fire on peaceful and unarmed marchers protesting a racial and religious curfew targeting Algerians and Muslims. The march by Algerian muslims itself broke the curfew. Fifty were killed, their bodies dumped in the river Seine. The police herded thousands of Algerian survivors into the same concentration camps they had used during the Vichy roundups of Jews twenty years earlier.

The French media (and police) ignored the murder of Muslims for thirty years, but splashed the murder of the French communists. Even so, the press colluded with the government to ensure that none of the police perpetrators were embarrassed. The government covered up, granting an amnesty in 1966 for the 1961 and '62 murders.

Apart from those protest marches that ended in death, the French police attacked many others causing injury. The reason behind these marches was Algeria's fight for independence, and France's repression, both overt and covert of that movement. Until de Gaulle's *volte face* in 1962, most of the French establishment and electorate assumed that Algeria would always be French, and that any amount of violence (against those

---

[51] The Charonne metro station. The march, protesting the behaviour of the illegal secret army terrorists of the OAS, and organised by the French communist party, was illegal. All protest marches in France need to be registered and approved by the prefect of police.

seeking independence) was acceptable. [52] The French students' union was the first trade union to organise for the independence of Algeria, or at least for a peaceful negotiation, which the French gave up in 1960. The students took to the streets to protest, and suffered vicious beatings. [53]

Papon was no stranger to violence, having used it extensively in putting down resistance to French rule in Morocco, and in Algeria during the war for independence, where he was prefect of police in Constantine. In a case of "almost industrial-scale torture", 108,175 Algerians passed through his interrogation centre at the Améziane farm on the outskirts of Constantine. [54]

---

[52] De Gaulle's announcement that France would pull out of Algeria led to the assassination attempt by the OAS, after which de Gaulle refused to support any more oppression of Algerians in France.

[53] Papon was replaced by the much more peaceful Maurice Grimaud, who had been present in the 1934 when the *Garde républicain*, Paris's own riot police, attacked fascists in the Place de la Concorde (the place of peace), killing 37 and leaving thousands wounded. This public relations disaster brought down the government and led to the incompetence of the French state during the years leading up to and during the Spanish Civil War, and the declaration of war against Germany. Grimaud vowed never to permit such carnage on the streets of Paris, and the 1968 May student protests and nationwide general strike passed without any deaths.

[54] To be fair to Papon, the torture centre was run by the army after the declaration of martial law and the handing over of civil power to the military. However, Papon was accused by many first-hand witnesses of participating in the enhanced interrogations, usually using the *gégène* hand-cranked electric generator attached to the victims' privates, ears, nose or fingers.

Even before Papon, French police had shot and beaten to death 6 Algerian-French citizens celebrating Bastille Day in 1953, along with a supporter from the CGT. [55]

In the 1940s, French troops murdered xx mutineers in Algeria

In 1944, they murdered at least 35 unarmed Senegalese *tirailleurs*, who were demanding their back pay before being demobilised, at Thiaroye near Dakar.

In 1945, they murdered thousands or even tens of thousands of Algerians in Sétif and Gueretta, admittedly after other Algerians had murdered Europeans in an orgy of celebration on VE-Day.

French police stood by as the population targeted supposed collaborators, lynching men and scalping women. The same police collaborated with the Gestapo, SD and Germany authorities during the occupation, sending 87,000 Jews to their deaths as well as a million to slave labour camps. Their leader in Bordeaux, the same Papon. Papon would eventually stand trial for the deaths of 1,560 Jews he shipped off to Auschwitz, but only at the end of a very long life. He served 3 years before being released on medical grounds, but still managed to hang on for another 5 years before succumbing.

USA

---

[55] The CGT, *Confédération Générale du Travail*, is the general workers' union for a long time associated with communism.

The US is the country that imprisons the greatest percentage of its citizenry, almost ten million people participating in the greatest tragedy of the 21st Century, so far. This dwarfs the prison system of the Third Reich.

Most prisoners are in the US prison system because of drugs. The USA prohibits its population from making individual decisions to become a drug addict, or to source privately or manufacture drugs without a licence. It does however, permit dangerous drug use if a government-approved doctor provides a prescription for a government-approved drug from a tax-paying corporation.

Drugs make many otherwise legitimate activities illegal. Importation, processing, buying, selling, using proscribed drugs is illegal and most offenses are felonies in the USA. [56] Felonies involve crimes that carry a year's prison sentence as a minimum, and can go as far as the death sentence. Their prosecution usually involves a jury trial with a lot of expense in trial lawyers, if the defendant can afford them, or the risk of conviction if he can't. [57]

Most crimes enforced in the USA are typical behaviours of Native Americans, African-Americans (Blacks) and Hispanics (either native born Americans or immigrants from Central and South America and the Caribbean). The Federal Bureau of Prisons no longer differentiates between Whites and Hispanics, in order to

---

[56] Almost half, 46%, the prison population is incarcerated following a conviction on drug offences. Statistics for incarceration in October 2020, 67,076 prisoners for drug offences out of 145,120 total. [141]

[57] Most incarcerations, 93.3% in October 2020, are of males,

minimise the allegations of favourable treatment to whites. [58]   Even so, the White+Hispanic prison population incarcerated in October of 57.6% underrepresents the 73% percent of the population that is White. The old definition of "non-Hispanic whites" is 60.7% in the national population, and only 27% inside, which explains why the BoP uses the "white" label.

Hispanics are a double curse on the prison system, with both native-born and immigrant Hispanics incarcerated. 30% of federal prisoners are Hispanics, 12% from outside, and 18% from inside the US, where the Hispanics form about 15% of the citizen population and almost 17% of the total population. Hispanics are better represented in the prison system than Native Americans, who make up 1.6% of the population but 2.4% of the federal prison population. African-Americans (Blacks) make up 38.5% of the federal prison population, but only 13.4% of the street population.

A predominantly white government, supported by Uncle Toms, will not make cheating on the golf course or the real estate market, or reckless driving, felonies. On the other hand, cattle raiding and smoking crack cocaine, relatively harmless crimes but common in Kenya or the Harlem, are punishable as felonies.

As in France and Britain, the focus on the criminal system is on ethnic minorities.   The psychological need for homage creates opportunities for those involved in law and order, but an ethnic minority

---

[58] It may be unfair to dwell on BoP populations, as the federal authorities only get involved in more serious crimes.

by its nature is vulnerable, lacks group support and is less likely to resist. Any resistance from such a vulnerable minority can be crushed more easily and with less regret. Any sign that a member of a minority has actually succeeded in society, in spite of his beginnings, and maybe showing a higher social position by clothing, car or attitude, is an even greater challenge to anyone in authority, and one that must be suppressed.

A demand for homage from the forces of law and order is the beginning of what can be a terrifying ordeal. The natural instinct to acquiesce to such a demand is confronted by a revulsion of oppression in cases of stop-and-search, or after repeated controls, or as the subject of racial abuse, all designed deliberately, if unconsciously, to stimulate resistance and permit a regression to violence.

Many victims never make it to prison. George Floyd died shouting "I can't breathe" as a police officer knelt on his neck, while three other officers stood around and did nothing to help him. That was 2020, and Floyd's death sparked off riots across America and around the world. However, George Floyd's death was nothing new.

Leading the protests was an organisation called *Black Lives Matter*. This movement started following the 2012 shooting of Trayvon Martin, and the acquittal of the community watcher who shot him. This acquittal effectively granted the right of anyone (not even an authorised police officer) to interfere in a person's business and shoot them dead if they don't let them. Whereas a police officer is sometimes authorised and sometimes justified to stop a citizen and interfere with their legal progress, a police officer has no authority to do so on a whim, or even a suspicion. In Martin's case, the intervening security guard had no authority to intervene.

Again, Trayvon Martin was not an isolated case. For those of an older generation, Rodney King was the first social media case of police brutality. King and his two friends were pulled over by police for reckless driving, and beaten as they left the car. King was spread-eagled on the bonnet of the car when the LAPD decided to take over the case from the CHP who were first on the scene. The senior LAPD officer ordered all to holster their guns, probably saving the life of King. It was, however, merely the start of a more serious beating. Filmed from a nearby balcony on 8mm film, King was beaten for ten minutes with taser and truncheons, while trying to escape the blows that continued. At times, the senior officer in charge ordered the beating to stop, and then he ordered more beating. Regardless of whether King had initially been resisting arrest or resisting restraint, after a minute of beatings, he was certainly entitled to try to escape a further illegal beating.

The film shown on TV led to the prosecution of the officers concerned, but not of the many other officers who stood by and watched. The acquittal of the police officers increased the feeling that there was neither justice for (black) citizens nor anything fundamentally criminal about committing crimes such as beating people up. The acquittal of the officers led to a spate of retaliatory crime by young blacks who, perhaps, were just looking for an excuse.

Police arresting other young blacks during the riots that following the acquittal were also filmed by amateur and professional cinemato- and photo-graphers. Initial police response was confused, sometimes heavy-handed and then when intelligent police officers realised that they were heavily outnumbered, passive, even allowing the theft of a police torch. Senior police officers were away on training courses or a political fundraiser, even though the timing of the acquittal was well-known and had been announced and planned to give police time to prepare for the expected trouble.

A white photographer was attacked and seriously wounded and other white or off-white passers-by suffered similar attacks. Protestors became rioters when they raided a liquor store. Other white journalists were attacked. Most of the violence came from just four black men; other black men looked after the injured and tried to help them out of trouble.

While the police did nothing, not even preventing traffic from reaching the riot zone, rioters looted gun stores. Police finally did do something, setting up roadblocks around the rich white areas of Beverley Hills, leaving the rioters free to loot what they could find elsewhere. The richest area left unguarded was Koreatown; when the firing started there, the police simply drove away. Koreans and African-Americans may have had poor relations, and these suffered more when an armed Korean shopkeeper killed a 15-year old girl suspected of shoplifting. Perhaps as a result, it was the area which suffered the worst damage, 45% of the looted stores were Korean-owned. Another third were Latino. White store owners got off lightly. The final score, along with thousands of burnt-out shops, was 63 dead.

The cause of all this, Rodney King, was a convicted felon on parole, and evading arrest on a potential drink-driving charge. The police had every right to stop and charge him, and would have done the community a favour if they had done so in a more circumspect manner. Beating a helpless man in the world capital of film was just asking for their behaviour to become live action news. Other incidents that led to LA riots also had their film and photograph witnesses, whose evidence circulated rapidly in an always-on TV culture.

The incompetent handling by the police of a simple arrest, and the incompetence generally of the US justice system, which both fails to reform the character of or rehabilitate those who fall foul of it, and fails to protect the community, is self-evident.

Rodney King was not the first African-American to suffer a beating at the hands of US law enforcement agents. For centuries, the forces of law and order have targeted them for punishment, for showing high spirits in any way, for singing and dancing in the streets, for "visual insubordination" or dumb insolence. [59] However, as a class they have suffered just as much from generalised racialist oppression and prejudice. Federal and state laws have prevented their gun ownership, while the lack of laws or enforcement have permitted differential pay and conditions, segregation, exclusion and harassment.

Perhaps the most eloquent critic of America's racial laws and culture was Martin Luther King, shot dead in 1968. The riots that followed his death left 43

---

[59] [177]

dead, three thousand injured and twenty thousand arrested.

Riots were nothing new to those campaigning for civil liberties. A year earlier, 85 people died in widespread riots led by those civil libertarians.

Federal and state laws did nothing to prevent the murders of Martin Luther King in 1966, or of the 4 young girls blown to bits by the Ku Klux Klan in 1964. It took 12 years to bring one the klansmen to justice, and 35 years to convict two others. The fourth died before he could be tried.

The FBIs reticence to prosecute klansmen was not similarly affected by the assassination of Malcolm X by members of the Black Muslim organisation, Nation of Islam; one assassin and two innocent bystanders were convicted.

Riots in America are nothing new. Every year or two years there are major riots in the United States, usually between African-Americans and the authorities, but also between white civilians and African-Americans, and other minority groups such as LBGT. The more famous or interesting include the Watts riots, the Long, Hot Summer, the Red Summer, the Zoot Suit riots, and the riots following Jack Johnson's victory in the heavyweight boxing championship. Rioting took place in the middle of the Second World War, as well as during First World War. Some are better known as massacres, where the minority groups never even got organised before the shooting started.

Abroad, the US has had a poor record in protecting anything other than its own capitalist interests.

In the 21st Century, the USA has started wars that have killed a quarter of a million people, and supports other countries waging wars in half a dozen countries, flaunting the Atlantic Charter and the foundation stone of the United Nations.

In the 1950s, 60s and 70s, the US financed and waged war in Indo-China, Vietnam, Laos and Cambodia, killing millions.

In the 1950s, the US waged war in Korea, killing millions.

In the 1940s, the US Army Air Force refused to bomb civilian targets, taking heavy casualties attacking well-defended industrial targets in Europe. However, with its reorganisation as the US Air Force, and the development of long-range bombers that could reach Japan, a new strategy was ordered by the government, similar to the British one in Germany. The 40 largest Japanese cities would be destroyed, their paper and wood houses attacked with phosphorus and napalm and, eventually, with two nuclear bombs. A million civilians died.

American war crimes during the Second World War were dwarfed by those of the Axis countries, but they are still enormous by any other standards. No single government organisation other than the communist governments of the Soviet Union and Red China and the fascist governments of Germany and Japan has ever killed as many civilians as the democratic government of the United States of America.

The basic motivation that drove most of these actions was a demand for homage to recover from the loss of face caused by Japanese or Communist success.

In both cases, they led to American economic losses, perhaps not deliberately.

Movements like Black Lives Matter, the Civil Rights, and many others have had some impact, in forcing the re-trial of brutal police officers, in enacting laws that provide rights or protection; meanwhile, conservatives have enacted laws to facilitate the prosecution of rioters and violent offenders, while police officers are every year better equipped to subdue the public, making it easier to kill, maim or beat them.

Many of the most violent offenders, police and civilian, are simply unintelligent, uneducated, suggestible people vulnerable to propaganda and lies pronounced by their own government and repeated in the media. Conspiracy theories, antagonistic broadcasts and religious tracts confuse the issue. It is rare to find an intelligent, well-read, polite person shot to death by the police, although Felipe Fernández-Armesto, an Oxford history professor, was beaten for arguing the legal niceties of jaywalking with his arresting officer.

The limited ability of government

If government exists to provide violent bigots with an opportunity to gain psychological points, it also offers showoffs a platform. The claims made by demagogues and propagandists hide a desultory success rate. The next misunderstanding is that of achievement. Governments are not designed to succeed, and citizens, voters and tax-payers vastly overestimate their ability to deliver on any project. The reasons are neither Machiavellian nor dualistic.

French history is populated by a century of lazy kings, the *rois faineants*. Historians called them lazy because they won few wars, and lost their empire. The lazy kings lost control of their empire to their prime ministers, the mayors of the palace who, did most of the work, started wars, fought the enemies of the state and became the Carolingian kings that followed them.

The reality is that, once on the throne, a king has little power to influence events. Those, who control access to the king, control what he learns and who he favours, and effectively control the country. It takes a particularly strong king and a peculiarly weak aristocracy to change this situation. There have been such kings and such aristocrats in history, but they rarely appear together. More common is the situation where both are strong, leading to civil war, such as during England's Barons War, or where both are weak, leading to invasion, for example, the Glorious Revolution.

Leaders of a nation's government are individuals. Very few have the skills or position and patronage to make others do what they tell them to do. The vast majority do what is attractive to them, keeps them in power, minimises the work they have to do, and brings sexual favours.

These individuals also have their own ideas. Barack Obama arrived in Washington determined to close down the Guantanamo prison camp. Donald Trump wanted to build a wall. Neither succeeded, a partial achievement was all that could be claimed optimistically. In reality, given the objectives they had given themselves, both failed, 100%. They both exerted themselves to achieve their goals, they had the support of their electorate and much of the civil service, yet both failed due to intransigence, wilfulness and the nature of organisations. Thousands of people benefit from the status quo and see no reason why they should lose their incomes just to support a politician's dreams of everlasting glory.

The only area of real independence that national leaders have is in foreign relations, including that of waging war. For a variety of reasons, this is an area of statecraft that has little control or oversight by the checks and balances of modern government.

Budgets are eventually overspent

the motley of clients, parasites, flatterers, men-at-arms, chamberlains, pages, chaplains, athletes, poets, painters, merchants, officials, secretaries, servitors, women, who were thronging into the audience-chamber [60]

No modern government makes money. Rarely did any old government.

"The present and the late king of Prussia are the only great princes of Europe, who, since the death of Henry IV of France, in 1610, are supposed to have amassed any considerable treasure. The parsimony which leads to accumulation has become almost as rare in republican as in monarchical governments. The

---

[60] Frederick Rolfe, Baron Corvo, describing the hangers-on at the Borgias' court in Rome, all desperate to eke out some subsistence without having to work for it. [143]

Italian republics, the United Provinces of the Netherlands, are all in debt. The canton of Berne is the single republic in Europe which has amassed any considerable treasure. The other Swiss republics have not." [61]

Charities are not allowed to make a profit, nor a loss. Businesses are obliged by their articles of association and by national regulation to make a profit, but 80% of those set up fail to do so within five years. Governments, on the other hand, are perfectly at liberty to make a profit, but never do. The few modern nation states that might claim to do so, Kuwait and Norway, for example, are making a profit by emptying their oil reservoirs, permanently depleting their national resources.

Any claim by any government that they are a rational choice for the entrustment of any activity that requires finance should bear in mind that they are the worst possible type of organisation to do that. Any alternative of charity or business is likely to do better.

A charity is just a tax-free business. It bluffs its employees into taking low or no wages, its suppliers into gifting them produce, and its customers to accept shoddy goods. Even so, it still cannot make a profit, and any potential is eaten up by the management and the massive marketing budget, which finances the steel and glass buildings of Madison Avenue, London, Paris but does little to provide fresh water to the starving of Africa. Only about 10% of any charity's received donations end up in the hands of the needy. The vast majority is spent on attracting more donations, or on

---

[61] [11]

supporting a wide range of other charities. So far, by 2020, no charity has ever closed down due a lack of need of its services, as a result of its successful operations. Therefore, charities are neither good targets for donation, nor achievers of clearly-set objectives. Anybody looking to relieve some social ill or resolve a problem should look at direct action instead.

Businesses have less moral leverage with employees, suppliers and customers, but are free to choose from a wider range of activities, including firearms, drugs, sports and gambling. Whereas charities are driven by their management, businesses are driven by their shareholders, who want a dividend or share growth in return for their investment. The purpose of business is to generate profit to pay these shareholders. There is no intrinsic need to satisfy customers, employees or government regulators.

Individual businesses and charities may, under the auspices of a particularly dynamic and altruistic individual, serve some greater social person. However, as soon as that person relinquishes command for whatever reason, the organisation will adopt the usual organisational behaviours.

Governments are different to charities and business. They do not bother attracting the finance they need to survive, or want to enjoy life, or seek to carry out their schemes. They merely take the money from those who have it, the tax-payers, or make the money by printing, or borrow it from those who should know better.

Tax-collection is inherent in human society, at least for 99% of the extant population. It is the essential behaviour that permits all of civilisation. Without taxation, there would be no concentration of cash, no investment in improvement, no technological advances, no human population of seven billion. *Homo sapiens* would still be an African ape with a species population of a few million, were it not for his ability to collect taxes.

Tax-collection has enabled the development of a complex society, in which individuals specialise in their activities depending on their natural inclinations, skills, locations and possessions. Specialisation enables greater production than that possible by an individual carrying out all the behaviours necessary for survival. As a result, the population of *Homo sapiens* now stands at over seven billion.

The guarantee of a permanent revenue stream from taxes permits tax-collectors to borrow money against it, further increasing the money available, to squander or to invest. Some of that money will usually result in increases of production, through improved communications, trade, technology or healthcare, and therefore will result in an increase in the economy, population and future taxes collected. This spiral of improvement does not necessarily happen in a unique tax society, but bounces from one to another. Those tax territories that are most tax efficient, that is, that collect the most taxes, in the most efficient manner, and spend it most wisely, will improve faster and further than the rest, and will conquer the rest, demographically or military.

Eventually, a tax society will survive only because of the money that its government can borrow. It is now two hundred years since the British and American governments paid off the debts they had incurred, one to defeat the French, the other to pay for independence from Britain. Since then, no major country has paid off its national debt.

Most humans borrow money to achieve specific objectives, such as to build a house. In traditional societies, newly-married couples incur a social debt by inviting their family, friends and neighbours to a communal house raising. This debt is then repaid by helping to build houses for the children of their family, friends, and neighbours. Similarly, money borrowed from a bank or building society in more urban societies is repaid from wages or salary during the course of a working life, or on their death with an insurance policy. There is no net gain.

Those who live their life in such ordered fashion may be admired by their neighbours and bankers, but there is a much better strategy to adopt in a competitive world.

It is much better for an individual to amass huge debts during his lifetime, enjoy living life to the full, and then die. Debts are one thing that children do not inherit, and those that enjoy the debtors' hospitality would hold him in high esteem. Bankers responsible for lending to such a man without the necessary collateral deserve the ignominy they would receive.

Governments, likewise can live prudently, or spend and die. Whether they spend their money wisely, on behalf of the tax-payer, or they squander it on wars and luxury for their cronies, affects greatly whether their eulogist would praise or criticise them, but government does not die, nor does their debt disappear with a change of government. Governments can default, print money to cause inflation, or just borrow more money, increasing taxes to pay the growing interest. The only alternative is to pay off the debt, but this rarely happens.

National debt is a huge pyramid scheme, a Ponzi scheme. It relies on an ever-increasing population of gullible investors along with stable market conditions. While such a population exists, the new investors in the scheme pay off the interest demanded by the older investors or creditors. Rarely can such investors pay down the capital, and mostly they just pay off the interest. The new investors merely increase the total capital debt. As the uninvested population decreases, in becomes increasingly difficult to attract investors, more of whom are needed. Higher rates of return may be advertised, further increasing the problem of repayment. This spiral of ephemeral promises merely increases the problems when the scheme comes to its inevitable end.

The every higher rates of return attract more investors, but repayment becomes increasingly difficult. Any downturn in the market that affects interest rates, cash flow or other investments will affect any Ponzi scheme, such as national debt. At some point, there will be insufficient investors to pay off the current debt repayments. The scheme will default or, if well managed, reschedule its debt. A believable front man and a gullible bank of investors can maintain a pyramid scheme for many years, through difficult market conditions.

Some countries manage to reduce their total national and local governmental debt. A rapidly-increasing population, the exploitation of natural resources, such as gold and diamonds, oil and gas, timber and metals, can create a long-term positive balance of payments and a better source of tax. A dedicated politician believing in fiscal prudency can help, but usually only as long as she is in power.

Even when there is a thrifty leader in charge of a nation's finances, and reducing the national debt is a political goal, there are immense pressures on government to continue spending beyond its tax revenues. Amazingly, when Australia managed to reduce its national government spending below its tax receipts, and reduced its need for borrowing to zero, it carried on borrowing money (selling government bonds) "in order to maintain the bond market", in other words, to provide tax-paid sinecures to financial market employees, managers, directors and shareholders. [62]

It is the inevitable end that governments will increase their taxes and debt. [63] Perhaps driven by a

---

[62] In order to spend this money, the government of the time, led by Howard and Peter Costello set up the Australian sovereign wealth fund known as the *Future Fund*. Costello is now the chairman of that fund and manages two hundred billion Australian dollars of assets, far less than the government's debt. His compensation for this part-time job was $230,417 in 2019. [146]

[63] From a list of European countries, the lowest debt-to-GDP ratio is Estonia, with 10% in 2017. Bulgaria managed to reduce its communist debt to 13%, operating a flat tax regime, but has recently allowed it to double to 26%. Luxembourg is the only other European country with such low relative debt. (States such as Jersey can have much lower debt as they have no foreign affairs or wars to manage, and their fiscal affairs are more likely to be managed directly by the tax-payers.) Some countries, like Ireland, Finland, Slovakia, Denmark, Lithuania, Latvia and Romania did manage to reduce their debt during the first decade of the 21st Century, but since the economic crisis of 2008 all their debt has risen to between 30% and 60% of GDP. All other European

temporary financial crisis or spending need, they will be unable to pay off the debt, and will default. [64]

What happens when a government defaults depends largely on circumstances, and partly on how this is presented. A blunt refusal to pay lenders is less harmful when there are other lenders that want to profit from the relationship that financing government offers. Genoese bankers were happy to step in when Philip II of Spain defaulted on his German bank loans.

Some governments just print more money. This usually leads to inflation, but in 2020 interest rates are near zero. Instead of allowing negative interest rates, which would upset rich people but would lead to falling prices for consumers, governments prefer to print money (quantitative easing, or QE, in the modern parlance), to maintain prices and keep the bankers happy.

In conclusion, no government, or government department, is inherently able to make a profit, or even

---

countries have seen a steady rise in debt with Belgium and the Mediterranean countries touching 100% or more.

[64] Government debt usually only measures national debt obligations, and ignores state and local government debt. Governments also have obligations which they should accrue for, but which they, unlike the businesses that they regulate, ignore. For example, pensions, healthcare and even salaries for workers that are almost impossible to sack, are costs that will be borne and therefore under GAAP accounting rules should be counted. Costs of military occupation, long-term programmes, whether of warships or hospital buildings, should also be included. Government obligations are so massive that they cannot do this without alerting the tax-payers and their financiers. As a result, government debt propaganda should be read as a simple way to compare one country's debt with another's, not as a guide to the absolute charge on tax-payers and their descendants.

break even. If tax-payers were investors, they should avoid governments completely, and ignore their propaganda prospectuses.

Governments can only operate while they maintain a monopoly of violence and are prepared to use it to enforce their taxes, and while the population is so used to these customary demands that they don't even notice them.

Every attempt by government to increase their sphere of action, their revenues or their expenditure should be resisted. There is always a better way of achieving any stated goal, and the usual best way is simply to do nothing, because no government will ever achieve its stated aims.

Interventions usually fail

The final popular misunderstanding about government is that, should do something, it would work. Activists, the media, opposition politicians and members of government often demand that government should do something. This call is usually nothing more than an attempt to occupy time and space and improve an individual's position in the organisation's hierarchy, but some will be misled into thinking that the government might actually be able to achieve the stated objective. This goes against all logic, history and scientific evidence.

Smith showed that any government intervention was inimical to the very objectives claimed for it. [65]

The normal process for deciding on government business should be successful in eliciting the facts, involving the stakeholders, and preparing the objectives. There are green papers for discussion, white papers for plans, discussion in committees and parliament, private thinking, articles and interviews in the media, and writing, books, pamphlets and academic papers.

However, this basic process is restricted in its effectiveness by the political bickering, between ministers, between parties, between those in favour and those against, between competitive contractors. It is finally ruined by the limitless funds available through taxation and the fact that there is a greater benefit for all involved, the greater the money that is spent.

The outcome of any government intervention is therefore that the budget will surpass the economic benefits.

Government intervention in emergencies, when the demands for action are the loudest, is even worse than the normal process. The process in emergencies is

---

[65] "It is thus that every system which endeavours, either, by extraordinary encouragements to draw towards a particular species of industry a greater share of the capital of the society than what would naturally go to it, or, by extraordinary restraints, to force from a particular species of industry some share of the capital which would otherwise be employed in it, is, in reality, subversive of the great purpose which it means to promote. It retards, instead of accelerating the progress of the society towards real wealth and greatness; and diminishes, instead of increasing the real value of the annual produce of the land and its labour." [11]

based around discussion alone, which is a poor process for decision making.

People might criticise the normal democratic process, which allows lobbyists to lobby, effectively bribing politicians. However, this is to misunderstand the lobby process. Anyone can lobby. Those that do are those that are most interested and willing to put the time, effort and money into the process. Those that sit at home and ignore the democratic process and then complain are going to complain whatever happens.

Regardless of whether the enemy is a Mexican immigrant, a coronavirus virion or an unelected bureaucrat in Brussels, government attacks on them are subconsciously only designed to elicit homage, service and contribution from the tax-payer, not the destruction of these dangerous agents. Indeed, any destruction would render the government unnecessary and their activities irrelevant.

We, the People [66]

The fault, dear Brutus, is not in our stars, but in ourselves [67]

If the public blames politicians and civil servants for society's ills, then the politicians and civil servants can equally blame the public. Clearly, in any democracy, the voters, the citizens and the tax-payers are responsible for the government they select. The people must question its own contribution.

Far outnumbering the members of government, the public has the ultimate power, both physical and financial, to decide the course of action, the behaviour of a state.

The public, however, rarely behaves in a rational, intelligent manner. Its behaviour is driven by prosaic affairs and governments know well how to channel their behaviour, in return for a few crumbs.

---

[66] The first 3 words of the Preamble to the Constitution of the United States, taking responsibility for the government of the territory. The Republic, as it is called, is made up of the People, not the people. The Romans made the same distinction, between the *Populus*, as in SPQR, *Senatus Populusque Romanus*, the people united in the political establishment through their representatives (equivalent to the government in terms of members of congress) and not the mob or the common people as individuals, rioting in the street or protesting a new tax, who would be the *vulgus*, or the plebs.

[67] Cassius, blaming the people for their servitude, in Shakespeare's *Julius Caesar*. [132]

Individuals are more interested in demarcation than improvement, more interested in being a big fish in a little pond than a small fish in a big pond. [68]

Changes in demarcation, the allocation of a certain position within the hierarchy of a social (non-kin) group, are effected not by covert, economic success, like a lottery win, but by competition between individuals in socially-accepted challenges, like a squash ladder or football league. For example, the theft of goods of cash may bring immediate financial rewards, but would not result in social promotion except within the den of thieves. Middle-class lawyers and doctors or other residents in posh areas will not invite nouveau-riche thieves or lottery winners to dinner just because they move in next door with wodges of cash.

In all this, humans reflect the mammalian heritage that they all have, along with that piscine ancestry which most would rather forget. The short attention span, shoal-swimming mentality of most is obvious to observers but rarely the observed. The protection that it offers makes for demographic success, but evolutionary collectivism.

There are, however, some behaviours that are uniquely human, which even our closest cousins, the other great apes, do not share.

---

[68] Good examples of human nature can be found in the history of the trades unions, the major organisations of the working classes. In spite of the socialistic idealism evinced by many who joined, the grim reality was that they strived for member pay increases first, demarcation second, and industrial survival not at all. There was rarely any attempt at solidarity between trades, co-operative action against the bosses or government, or to create the economic growth to attract new and younger members. [172] [56]

The most obvious is the submission to authority. Not only does the public kow-tow to almost anybody wearing a suit, a uniform or carrying a clipboard, but it gives them the fruits of its labour, even all the fruits, with hardly a complaint. Even worse, is the liberal bleating that justifies such craven behaviour, and the praise heaped on the perpetrators of this heinous crime.

Psychologists are starting to investigate taxation as a financial transaction, mainly with a view to facilitating the extraction of more money. They have not started looking at the submission to authority in anything other than the most obvious fashion. The biggest failure is to recognise that taxation is not a financial transaction, but a non-kin male interaction. Once this is understood, everything else follows.

The first stage of taxation is the demand for homage, but it requires and usually receives an instinctive behaviour from the victim, without which human society would not exist.

Acquiescence

The first and most important trait that humans have, which is unknown among wild animals, is to acquiesce to strangers. All wild animals acquiesce to orders, instructions, directions from those they know, their parents, uncles and aunts, brothers and sisters, cousins, regarding stranger danger, food and salt sources, food and drink, and sleeping arrangements. Sometimes, there will be arguments about mating, but these are usually sorted out by violence.

However, at no time will an adult male wild mammal permit a strange wild adult male to enter its territory, mate with its females or partake of the food and drink available therein.

Humans, on the other hand, will, under certain conditions, permit strangers to enter their territory, take their food and drink, and even to mate with their females or at least dictate when they can mate. This acquiescence is essential to create the complex societies in which humans live, with many unknown people and frustrating interactions, which would otherwise result in violence, actually leading to improvement in society.

The conditions in which males will not acquiesce include new strangers, new demands, or significant changes in the demands, or in adolescence or drunkenness.

In a tax society, tax-collectors, agents of government, come, often unannounced, and take 10% of a citizen's produce, once a year or monthly. In addition, agents will stop citizens as they go about their business, crossing rivers or bridges, using roads, buying or selling, building a house or getting married, registering a child or burying a parent. The citizen acquiesces to all these interventions, usually without even noticing.

Any one of these interactions with a strange male would result in a violent altercation in any other species of animal, and in a predator or ape, would probably result in serious injury or death. In humans, all that results is a confirmation of the relationship between a tax-collector and a tax-payer, between an agent of government and a citizen.

Acquiescence is an active verb. The act of acquiescing to government demands can be conscious, unconscious, automatic but noticed, or subconscious, automatic and unnoticed. Once acquiescence starts it is difficult to stop it. Acquiescers are one more individual in the group of acquiescers, and the group of resisters is one short. Peer pressure is powerful, so is custom. Children growing up who acquiesce will continue for the rest of their lives, at least until they reach grumpy old age. However, it is possible to stop acquiescing and to start resisting. Conscious decision makers can also decide to resist.

Selection of behaviour depends on instinct, upbringing, peer pressure, emotions, the choice and associations with each choice, perceived benefits, direct and indirect, sexual and economic. At some point, the decision maker can make a choice between two options based on the benefits, and might make these benefits public. However, most people will make the wrong decision based on their public declarations.

This is not evolutionarily important selection. This is only the selection by an individual, not a mathematically-significant group of people, whose behaviour will affect the evolution of a species.

For example, in the COVID, Brexit, Trump triad, the best decision that Trump supports who want to Make America Great Again, clean out the swamp and reduce government interference in government would have been to have voted for someone else, anyone else. On the other hand, the best decision that a democrat looking to increase the role of government, the range of services offered to minorities and the vulnerable, and

Acquiescence is easy while the demands maintain demarcation. Resistance is preferred for any change to the status quo, not to the absolute economic or social standing, but to the relative position. Therefore, governments can easily introduce measures that extend inequality, or even that reduce it. Subversion, the introduction of ethnic or religious minorities in between established layers in society can lead to pogroms, religious wars or even civil wars against the government.

The combination of a demand for homage and acquiescence permits further taxation, demands for service and a financial or production contribution. In exchange, the government will permit the payer of homage to carry out his trade, to marry and raise a family, and may from time to time protect him and his property from vandals, bandits and pirates.

However, not all non-kin interactions start with demands for homage. Two businessmen meeting for the first time are not interested in the unidirectional exchange of taxation, but they can still benefit from the innate behaviour of acquiescence. Instead of the mammalian fight/flight/freeze, they can trade goods, services and cash. Equally, a suitor can join the marriage market in a neighbouring town without having to kill his future father-in-law.

Acquiescence to limited demands for homage, service and contribution generally lead to improvements and a growing economy and demography. Paying homage is usually an unconscious or at least an uncontrolled act, but the benefits are obvious. Acquiescence provides genetic and often financial advantages. Members of a group or hierarchy can profit from government monopolies, sinecures, tax breaks and contracts, while they are better protected and mostly avoid the pointless violence of government agents.

It is not just kings, presidents, prime ministers, ministers and their enforcers who demand homage. Most humans share this behaviour, even if they rapidly learn whom to demand homage from to avoid a beating. Citizens reminding police officers who pays their salaries learn this lesson quickly.

Most critical behaviour in complex societies and large organisations, including modern civilisation itself, is a superior in a hierarchy demanding homage from a subordinate, and the reciprocal payment of homage to the superior. Complaints about one's superiors or inferiors are rarely important behaviours affecting demography, and usually just excuses invented after the fact to defend against the inevitable attacks by colleagues who would label such behaviour collaboration or appeasement, or oppression.

One final motivation for citizens to pay homage to the powerful is peer-pressure, especially when it consists of blind adulation.

Adulation

Tax-payers do more than just acquiesce to taxation and the government enforcers, they actively vote for them, even when faced with evidence that they are murderers, thieves, cheats, torturers, adulterers, and frauds. Like heroes, their foibles merely entertain the electorate.

The adulation voiced by the public for even the scaliest politician is illogical except when looked at in evolutionary terms. All mammals imprint on their parents and on those who they see in the first years of their lives. Images that represent kings and queens, presidents and popstars may adorn stamps, coins, scout huts, offices, ships, and sitting rooms. The constant repetition of the same image bores its way into any suggestible new-born brain. Ideas as well as images can form similar points of reference in the human brain, which forms as a result of its inputs. By the time a brain reaches adolescence, it is programmed for certain behaviours.

All social mammals also exist within hierarchical communities, in which the alpha male or female is dominant and all subordinates pay it homage. It is not sufficient to acquiesce to the boss, there must be a visible, costly and pointless exercise to admit it. This adulation is easily confused with gushing praise, a worthless gewgaw, but it is much more important than it appears. Adulation leads to false sense of security on the part of the recipient, and its incessant repetition leads to a false sense of reality on the part of the adulator. The necessary kow-towing to a more powerful adult may be necessary when young, alone and vulnerable, but is no longer necessary when mature and friendly. The confusion leads to the acceptance of a worthless aging and perhaps toothless president or king who could be knocked off his throne by a young Turk.

The worst moment in a government's life is election, and it is at this moment that the electorate has the greatest opportunity to voice its disapproval of government. Instead, it votes for it. Even if it votes for an opposition party, it is still voting for a party that will maintain 99% of the taxes and 99% of the laws, in other words, 99% of the government of the predecessor, and will add more taxes and more laws during its existence.

Instead, the public treat its politicians like lovers, with obsession, supporting their peccadilloes, creating superstar leaders who feel responsible to no-one, that they have a right to commit any crime.

Adulation of public figures is an established mammalian behaviour. Babies imprint on the most important figures in their upbringing, and mammals reinforce this result throughout life. Whoever occupies time and space becomes important for the observer. Whoever occupies time and space the most becomes a natural leader. Modern media technology merely increases the public for any individual. Without it, individuals were forced to travel or communicate their presence through stories, heraldry, castles, bridges, roads and vassals of questionable loyalty.

Anyone who dominates time and space is the focus of attention for anyone watching. They love, they believe and they repeat whatever is said, and will even kill others who don't.

Associate

Citizens are even more responsible for the biggest problem to face modern society, the proliferation of government jobs. When a government taxes at 10%, it is unlikely that more than 10% of the population are employed in collecting and disbursing the money. However, when taxes are at 50% or more, then it is probable that much more than half the population is working for the government.

Other potential tax-payers, rather than staying to work hard and contribute to society with their work and taxes, leave to live on a tax-haven, or simply work on the black market and pay no taxes at all. Even worse are those tax-payers who join the hierarchy and become tax-collectors.

Every traitor who becomes a tax-collector not only reduces the tax take by his contribution of 10% of his salary, necessitating a doubling of tax on his best friend, but he increases the demands by 100% of his new salary, requiring another 10 friends and family to double their contribution. This imbalance explains why increases in the government headcount are so disastrous for any economy.

Cash in the private economy can only be invested in luxury or improvement. Cash in the public economy can be invested in foreign or civil war, or in buying votes through the takeover of existing private businesses such as coal and steel, transport, utilities, medical services, or even recruitment.

While government headcounts are small, their ability to extract taxes from the economy is also small. Most of the profits of a year's work are reinvested in businesses. When a government headcount, including all the unemployed, recipients of social security, doctors and nurses, teachers, soldiers, law enforcement officers, civil servants and politicians reaches half the population, the retired and working population has to pay with their work all their salaries and expenses, as well as the equipment and infrastructure.

The decision to join the civil service or to take a tax-paid sinecure such as unemployment benefit, while immediately and temporarily gratifying, causes lasting and permanent damage to the economy. Not only does it encourage others to do the same, with increased motivation, but it leaves the economy weaker than before. Whatever the reasons for joining the government, the government itself is weaker, too, as it controls a bigger slice of a smaller pie, but the big slice is now divided by an even bigger crowd trying to eat it. That is one reason why, as the economies of countries founder, those who reach the top positions of political power are no longer the captains of industry and major landholders, but minor members of trades unions, failed professionals, and sons of immigrants. These representatives of the people are just as responsible for the continuing decline of the economy as they increase the tax rate, government intervention and the government headcount. Blaming the government for ills is no longer possible when the person blaming it is a member.

Attack

The few net tax-payers who remain outside the government's control find fewer and fewer ways to communicate their belief that hard work and low government intervention are the only ways to achieve a strong economy and fund government. As red tape, covert taxes, inspections, extortion, lockdowns and closures, add to the misery, letters to MPs, interviews on local television or trade association meetings are no longer sufficient to effect positive change, or even to prevent negative change. The tsunami of government interference is just too powerful.

The end result is that those who are disenfranchised, set aside or left behind take to the streets to protest. Defending themselves against any act of frustration merely increases the expense of government. Riots destroy infrastructure which needs repair and replacement with more expensive, vandal-proof glass. Insurance premiums rise. Worse, governments feel threatened, and increase funding for the police and army, further increasing taxes. At best, a government may pass some laws to calm rioters, but these are usually ephemeral and have little effect. [69]

The lack of respect of government agents and the police leads step by step to the removal of the inhibition that taxation uses to prevent mindless or wilful violence. Once removed, either gradually or more usually in a fit, perhaps encouraged by propaganda, a herd instinct, the violence is unleashed against any symbol of authority.

---

[69] Rioters claimed victory in the British Poll Tax Riots of 1990. However, the poll tax proposals were withdrawn and replaced with the much less-fair Council Tax, which also collected twice as much in taxes. The rioters lost. There are few modern riots which have led to long-term improvements. The collapse of the communist states was already prepared long before the rioters hit the streets, and it is questionable who actually benefited from the change. The Arab Spring resulted in temporary changes, but it is not clear if they led to any significant improvements. Only in Tunisia, a relatively well-off country, did it bring any real change. In the poorest countries, it merely led to civil wars, which continue in Syria, Yemen, Libya and Iraq.

Vandalism and graffiti are the most obvious examples of the gradual erosion of trust between a citizen and his (local) government but petty theft and shoplifting are similar. They have no financial motive, just revenge against the system that promises but fails to deliver.

Propaganda is particularly effective. Governments brainwash their citizens in the months leading up to a war, depersonalising, demonizing the enemy and anyone who treats with him. There is little difference in their behaviour against foreign or internal enemies. Media brainwashes their customers with a particular political goal. Public and media outcry over the vandalism and destruction gives the politicians the power to implement ever-more draconian measures.

The greater the resistance to taxation, therefore, the greater the taxation, and the greater the destruction of genes that discourage acquiescence.

The 7 Bad Habits of Highly Destructive People

Left to their own devices, the human population will demand homage from those it sees as weak and vulnerable, and seek service and contribution. It will rarely raise sufficient power to extract much more than a tiny percentage of the economy for its own nefarious purposes. Most taxes raised have to be locally spent, if only because they are locally raised.

Once a foreign power occupies a territory, however, the situation changes. The new government feels oppressed, and needs to protect itself from those who resist the occupation. A foreign occupier is a good advert which attracts other foreign occupiers. Given the chance, they will ask the citizens to contribute to their defence. Nobody in their right mind would ever finance a continued oppressive occupation. They therefore have to prepare the ground by inventing fictitious or real enemies, who will come and destroy, kill, rape and steal.

The major reason that politicians and governments are able to oppress citizens and their own electorate is that the public, especially that part vocal in the media of communications, complains and demands action against these foreign threats. Where this clamour is loud enough, politicians oblige. They use their own rhetorical powers to increment the enthusiasm for action, creating the conditions for draconian actions.

What, then, can be done to avoid this and prevent such an escalation ? The first step is to recognise the public clamour for what it is, wind. In this chapter, the major observable behaviours that channel support for political action are defined, using the format found in transactional analysis (TA), the interaction between two human beings.

It may be useful to recognise the behaviours that lead us to panic unnecessarily and to ignore real problems. It may be profitable if we can instead act according to our intelligence, to hoard or sell before the panic. It may even be possible to limit our own such behaviour and even train others to limit the effect of such panics.

Some of these behaviours are typical mammalian ones, others are common in primates, while a few are restricted to humans. All are relevant in kin groups, for interactions between adults, between children and adults, between children, and also in non-kin groups. As such, they are much more widely used than the behaviour of taxation, which is restricted to non-kin male interactions.

Behaviour is not demand and acquiescence, the unique behaviour of humanity. But individual herd behaviour, all animals and mammals do these things. Repetition is improved due to human stamina, but other animals repeat behaviour, apes copy, answer (bot not question), ignore and confuse.

The difference between taxation and these behaviours is that taxation is a forced interaction between two people, without which there is no opportunity for improvement. These 7 behaviours are individual ones. There is often a victim, but there is no intrinsic obligation in the behaviour of one. Human nature perhaps encourages one or other behaviour, but they are all subject to rational observation, critical judgement and avoidance.

The 7 habits are not intrinsically good or evil. Duality has no place here. Nor should their perpetrators receive labels of stupid or ignorant, evil or malicious, brave or fortunate. The behaviours are inherent in our genetic make-up, shared throughout the human species and all humans behave in these ways at times.

For most of the time, these behaviours support the economic and demographic growth of human society. Only rarely, and usually once the effective tax rate surpasses 10%, do these behaviours become destructive.

Ignore

All cleverness . . . was in itself suspicious [70]

The first bad habit is to ignore the available sources, which could help to make a correct decision. These include learning opportunities from personal experience (forgetting), from others (isolating) and from the environment (ignoring). This isolation from information bases the selection of a course of action completely on luck. At best, selecting between two courses of action, the right decision will be made in only half the cases. With more options, the right decision will be selected with even less frequency.

In order to make a correct decision, all factors affecting it need to be considered, a cost-benefit analysis. These factors include the list of all those affected, how they will be affected, the cost and benefit to different groups. In addition, objectives and points of view are necessary. Most of this information is readily available, if sought out.

This habit exists because in itself, isolation is useful. It permits an individual to concentrate on a certain activity, without interruptions or time spent investigating. As a child, isolation is detrimental in many ways, but adults can survive happily with what they have learnt, and may not need any additional input. Adult wild mammals often live in an isolated state, where they cannot learn from anyone else, and

---

[70] George Eliot describing the English (rural) propensity to ascribe performance to magic rather than preparation, training, practice, and physical and mental acumen. [150]

older classes of animals are even more likely to live a solitary life.

Habit - Ignore

Behaviour

Posit a single statement, unsupported and usually unverifiable or erroneous, to argue a particular belief or course of action.

Making decisions without defining *who* will do *what* and at what *cost* to *whom*.

Roles

Ignoramus

Outcomes

The ignoramus maintains his belief even when faced with facts, and otherwise convincing philosophical arguments.

Outcome

Usually wrong decisions.

Interpretation

Forgetting is an important part of human nature, allowing sufferers to overcome physical difficulties without long-term psychological damage.

From difficult experiences, pleasures are remembered while pain and cost are forgotten. Forgetting reduces the motivation to avoid such experiences in the future. While the benefits to the population of such behaviour through the process of procreation are obvious, they work equally well in sport, business and war.

The ignoramus has unexpressed reasons for his behaviour and selects an appropriate belief that supports them, or a fact that avoids having to discuss them.

This behaviour is the one that requires least thought or positive action; it is also the one that will produce the least benefit. The individual who ignores despises himself and others.

Alternative behaviour

Comparison, discovery, remembering times past.

While this behaviour is self-harming, it harms others when they listen to, copy and repeat it. The best thing is to ignore it. Even repeating it to criticise gives more publicity than it deserves.

It should be noted that it is perfectly acceptable for one person to ignore someone because they talk rubbish, because who-does-what-to-whom-for-what-reason is already defined. The observable behaviour that should be avoided is that of a commander ignoring the commanded and the impact of their actions.

Identification

Ignoramuses use abstract nouns to describe their subjects, rather than active verbs, proper nouns describing groups rather than individuals executing specific behaviours, and conditional terms such as could, should, would and up to, as much as, without ever making specific comparisons.

They maintain their belief even when confronted by facts, even reinforcing their belief (belief perseverance) rather than changing it.

The best option is to ignore the ignoramus until he requests information.

Copy

Copying is one of the fundamental mammalian actions. Academics may divide it into imitation and emulation, cognitive and social, conscious and unconscious.

Another synonym is *to ape*, with good reason, for it is a typical trait of the great apes and many other primates, when it is known as "monkey see, monkey do". [71] Copying is instinctive, unlike some of the actions that people copy, although it can also be deliberate, to create a sense of empathy (as a salesman, psychologist or possible sexual partner), or to annoy (as a colleague, a psychopath or a failed sexual partner).

Copying is the first sign of intelligence, the ability to learn behaviour that is not innate. Copying allows us to pick up all the culture of our parents' generation without doing any of the intellectual work.

However, copying destructive behaviour is inherently dangerous.

---

[71] [173]

Habit - Copy

Behaviour

The first person carries out some behaviour. A second person observes the behaviour and copies it to the best of his ability.

Roles

Performer
Copier

Outcomes

The performer succeeds in the replication of his behaviour without recourse to threats or rewards. Performers create groups made up of their copiers, or followers.

Interpretation

The copier claims membership of the group dominated by the performer, but usually as an inferior.

Alternative behaviour

Refusal.
A refusal to copy behaviour is a clear statement of rejection of the performer and his group. It is, however, the only way to create original ideas, with the possibility that others will copy and join this new group, initially in an inferior position.

Identification

Blind copying, imitation, is inherently dangerous. Only the observation of results, the calculation of cause and effect, and the execution of an appropriate behaviour to achieve a desired result can lead to profitable copying. [72]

The identification of dangerous behaviour can best be achieved by a simple question, such as "What are you trying to achieve ?" If the answer to the question is not a simple measurable quantity from a SMART objective, then it is likely not a behaviour worth copying. If the answer is an angry outburst, then the behaviour is dangerous.

Another way is to use the Socratic filter. Is it true ? Is it positive ? Is it useful ?

In either case, the situation forces a conscious and intellectual consideration before any dangerous copying.

Herd behaviour

Copying in a herd can rapidly spread useful and dangerous behaviours.   A member of a herd copies the majority of the other members. [73] Copying is instinctive, even if the behaviour copied is inherited.

---

[72] This is now called emulation in academic circles.

[73] This behaviour is confirmed by the Asch conformity experiment, which has been carried out many times in different social situations. A lone voice will agree with a wrong assertion 37% of the time, but only 5% of the time if someone else voices a correct assertion. A large proportion, 25% of the population, will ignore the herd and assert correctly. This large number probably

The latest panic over coronavirus is a good example of human herd behaviour. Even while many people recognise it as a panic, and recognise that their behaviour is irrational, they accept it, carry on with that behaviour, and demand similar behaviour from others.

Even intelligent people, who practise daily the ability to collect data, analyse it, and decide on a course of action most favourable to their personal and group objectives, follow the herd blindly.

Not all people are so blind as to copy any behaviour. A quarter of individual members of a group, 25%, will refuse to copy banal or false claims outright. However, 5% will always copy them without recognising them as false. Individuals will copy a false premise 37% of the time. [74]

Independence of thought is increased with active support from other group members, indicating that the best way to brainwash someone is to isolate them. Through a process of exclusion, isolation and forced repetition, demagogues can create a large crowd of angry protestors.

All the evidence necessary to discard it as a panic exists but people ignore it. Popular exhortations

---

indicates a lack of predators. Large herbivores that behave in this way will suffer increased predation, however, lone adult primates are not usually targeted by predators, perhaps due to their aggression, their lack of flight instinct which drives predator attack instincts, their use of weapons, their height or at least their standing posture which confuses or subdues them, and their diurnal habits. Leopards do regularly take sleeping nightwatchmen.

[74] These numbers come from the Asch conformity experiments.

to help defeat the virus, to protect the vulnerable or to flatten the curve are all good indications that this behaviour should not be copied. The use of statistics to improve the attraction of these behaviours is also misleading. The measurable objectives need to relate to the individuals carrying out the behaviours, not for the virus.

Copying can be conscious imitation, or unconscious mirroring (isopraxism). Birds and primates mirror. Humans mirror from a very early age. Mirroring helps to develop both skills and empathy. Deliberate copying helps in the same way. Even if the copying is an attempt at ingratiation and both parties understand the falsity, it still works. However, mostly, mirroring works when the copier wants to improve his relationship with the performer. Consciously or unconsciously, he mirrors the behaviour. Thus, copying is an important social interaction.

Role in Success

If the behaviour promotes economic or demographic growth, copying is beneficial to the individual and to society.

Copying is much more efficient than intellectual learning, both in time and energy consumed. Animals that copy, primates especially, are able to adapt to changing circumstances, even while their genes remain the same.

Children learn their behaviour by copying their parents, especially their mother. They learn language by copying her, hence the term *mother tongue*. Children also learn from their siblings, colleagues, books, TV, digital media and as adults they learn from their colleagues.

If the performer is a politician, his motivation is to stay in power or to increase it. Copying the behaviour of a politician may help the copier stay in his position or increase his personal power, but it will have the greatest effect in keeping the politician in power.

The most effective copiers are those who work in the media, who can promulgate the acts of the performer while becoming a performer themselves. The gain in their readership can help them keep their jobs or win promotion.

Much of the power of the media comes from communicating culture through stories. The media performers have millions of watchers, readers and listeners who can copy their messages.

An effective tool for politicians and the media is fear. When the media support the politicians and the public support the media, becoming effectively members of the press and performing the same fear-raising acts, then panic can set in. Politicians, the media and the public react in illogical and harmful ways, usually detrimental to the economy and the health and safety of the public

Role in Failure

Whatever the cost [75]

Looking at the cost, it is important to recognise that everything has to be paid for.

Brexiteers have said this time and time again, as have politicians implementing lockdown, travel restrictions and mask wearing. Trump's policies to make America great again ignore the cost. The WHO guidance on COVID specifically warns against any lockdown or mass programme without doing such an analysis.

Any behaviour that incurs a cost should not be copied blindly. Sacrificing social and civil liberties, health and lives are major costs. Copying others' calls for such restrictions or implementing them is a dangerous behaviour.

---

[75] A popular cry by politicians and activists supporting Brexit and COVID measures, but one which, in the English language, goes back to John Donne. Winston Churchill had used the phrase in his "We shall fight on the beaches" speech, and a similar terminology, *at all costs*, in his "blood, toil, tears and sweat" speech. A fortnight later in "their finest hour" speech, he dreamed of a thousand year empire (*reich* in German), but the war would cost Britain its empire, and the world 60 million lives. Sacrificing everything may look glorious, but it is no way to prepare for a long-term future.

Repeat

If you always do what you always did, you will always get what you always got [76]

Repetition can function on any innate behaviour, but also on learned behaviour, where it functions as a multiplier. Any beneficial behaviour will benefit the performer.

Stereotypy in animals, common in captivity, such as the tiger pacing its cage, is usually the sign of a problem. Few animals persist in any behaviour longer than necessary to achieve immediate satisfaction. While young may play, adults do not. It may be that human repetitive ability is a form of animal stereotypy, effectively a pathology, perhaps due to the process of domestication or social living, either of which would restrict behaviour.

Humans also repeat, even when it makes little sense; 97% of people when confronted by a new problem will carry on doing the same thing, only 3% will think about the problem and try to figure out an alternative strategy. [77]

In productive humans, repetitive behaviour is highly profitable. Repetition allows for mass production, travel, the creation of wealth, and can lead to a division of labour.

---

[76] Popularly attributed to Albert Einstein, but first recorded only in 1981, in a conference in Milwaukee.
[77] [174]

Like copying, however, repetition without thought can lead to the mass production of unwanted goods, or destructive behaviours.

Finally, blind repetition prevents the repeater from improving or optimising the process.

Habit – Repeat

Behaviour

One person acts repetitively.

Roles

Repeater

Outcomes

The repeater produces as much as possible.

Interpretation

Repetition of innate, learned or copied (inherited) behaviour is the rejection of originality.

Alternative behaviour

A refusal to repeat will result initially in lower production and more spare time. The repeater can invest this time in creatively optimising or even automating the process, leading to greater productivity at lower cost.

Repetition

Copying alone is a powerful tool that has helped mammal and bird species succeed. However, copying alone is not as powerful as copying and repeating. A bird's incessant repetition of its favourite song, calling for a mate, or a mammal's repeated braying of a political statement, to the exclusion of anyone else, any logical debate, any pause for thought is responsible for much of that individual bird or mammal's success.

Repetition is an effective learning mechanism.

The human facility for copying and repeating allows mass control through a process of public declamation. Religions, political parties, movements ring out their catchphrases and demand repetition.

Question and Answer

When you question, it slows you down [78]

There are many kinds of questions, and the type of questions we ask can make the difference between a growing economy and a dwindling empire. There are questions which we ask ourselves, the signs of doubt, the seeds of discovery. Then there are the questions we ask others, signs of ignorance or confidence,

---

[78] Francis 7, criticising Logan 5 for questioning the system, in the film, *Logan's Run.* [145]

Habit – Question and Answer

Behaviour

One person demands from another person a reply. The other person answers the question.

Roles

Asker
Responder

Outcomes

The asker reinforces his position of superiority over the responder.

Interpretation

This can be a simple demand for homage, a form of recognition, or of recognition of superiority. The best outcome for a responder who answers the questions is merely to maintain the status quo. The best outcome for a responder is not to answer the question, but to ask another question.

Alternative behaviour

By not answering the question, the responder can increase his relative status, and both asker and responder can benefit.

Lose Questions

Lose questions are those by which the asker wishes to maintain or gain superiority over the respondent.

The only benefit that pertains to a lose question answered is to the asker. There is no benefit to the responder, regardless of whether he is right or wrong; usually, he is wrong, but he may think he is right.

Before the lose question is answered, the respondent may know more than the asker. Afterwards, the asker has improved his position by gaining knowledge, but the respondent's position is weakened as the value of his knowledge is diminished through dissemination.

Usually, however, the lose question is a trick question. The asker knows the answer he is looking for already; he is looking for and will not accept any other answer, even if it is theoretically correct.

Regardless of the benefit for the respondent, there is always a greater benefit for the asker.

Is there benefit for the respondent ? If he satisfies the asker, then he may receive a reward as a subordinate, but he may also receive more questions as a result. The key point is the relationship of superior to subordinate. A subordinate ((worker) asking for advice from a superior (boss) maintains the position of subordinate. A superior (teacher) checking the knowledge or skill of a subordinate (student) maintains the position of superior. The only beneficial behaviour for the responder is to refuse to answer the question. The subordinate will have to work out the answer for himself, taking on responsibility and developing as a human being, while the student can concentrate on more useful pedagogic experiences.

Therefore, the correct answer to the question "What is the capital of Albania ?" is a gain question such as "What's in it for me if I answer, and what more will I get should I answer correctly ?" The wrong answer to the question is "Tirana".

Gain Questions

Gain questions are those by which the asker wishes the respondent to gain knowledge or to increase his self-worth.

Asking gain questions transmits some of the asker's power to the respondent. In doing so, he loses something, which needs to be replaced, usually by the respondent in turn asking gain questions.

Asked a gain question, the respondent is forced to ask himself a question and then to answer it himself or ask a gain question in turn.

The correct answer is to ask oneself "How can I profit from this opportunity ?" The key point is that the asker silences himself by his own question, and the respondent is now in charge of time and space.

For example, a teacher could ask a student, "How would you set up this experiment ?" The student would have to ask himself the question "How would you set up the experiment ?" and then work out the process. The best answer would eventually be of the form "My way would be to .... Can you think of any ways to improve the set up ?" or "Are there any areas that you think I have failed to consider ?"

The student should not answer the question if he already knows how he would set up the experiment; his ideas may be wrong. He should instead set up the experiment.

Answers

The best way to find out things, if you come to think of it, is not to ask questions at all. [79]

Knowledge in itself has no value. Given purpose, some facts are useful, and those who possess them may profit. Restricted information is worth more than that in the public domain. Secrets change in value as a function of supply and demand, in the same way as any other commercial good. However, facts are facts. Once discovered and widely communicated, their intrinsic value is nil. Modern technology provides easy access to information, so the ability to memorise data, or to prove this skill by answering questions, is no longer valuable in itself.

---

[79] If you fire off a question, it is like firing off a gun; bang it goes, and everything takes flight and runs for shelter. But if you sit quite still and pretend not to be looking, all the little facts will come and peck round your feet, situations will venture forth from thickets and intentions will creep out and sun themselves on a stone; and if you are very patient, you will see and understand a great deal more than a man with a gun. Another great observation about observation from Elspeth Huxley. [22]

The most counter-intuitive behaviour of destructive people is to answer other people's questions. Lost people ask for directions; confused people ask for clarification; sufferers ask for comfort; the worried ask for reassurance; children seek knowledge. It seems natural to answer their questions. Intelligent people answer questions; helpful people answer questions; kind people answer questions; teachers build a career around answering questions; parents feel good when they answer their children's questions; pub quiz team members feel great when they answer questions. What could possibly be the problem with answering questions ?

Helping does not help

Asking questions is a major differentiator between human beings and all other animal life. While other mammals are good at providing information, none so far are capable of asking for it. [80] This ability to ask allows humanity to create complex societies by checking whether others understand or follow the critical processes for social interaction.

Answering questions, however, is of more value to the person asking than to the person answering. Answering questions reinforces the natural superiority of the asker. He is delegating the trouble of finding out, or testing the knowledge level with an assumption that it is lower than his own. The asker

---

[80] Dogs can ask to go for a walk, to eat or for a cuddle, not for information. They cannot cope with concepts like the delay between now and when they will go for a walk. Like children under the age of 2 years, they live only in the present.

remains in control of the conversation. He can criticise the responder, even if the responder answers correctly. He can follow up with another, harder question, and keep on asking until the responder fails, gets angry or gives up, at which point he will have lost the interaction.

Police officers, military interrogators, headmasters ask questions; criminals, prisoners of war, recalcitrant schoolchildren answer them. There is a psychological benefit to the asker, a loss to the answerer. The exchange of information is of no value <u>in itself</u>. The information is not important, just the human behaviour, the identification of the dominant and the submissive.

It is human nature to answer questions. Obligatory schooling reinforces nature. The simplest teaching is lecture and question. However, question and answer systems are rarely the best methods of learning, and learning facts is overrated as an activity.

Outside formal education, questions and answers provide rapid solutions to everyday situations.

From an early age, human children are taught to be helpful, trained, rewarded. If they want attention, they know that they can get it by helping others. Humans learn quickly that the best way to get a dog's attention is to offer it food; a dog will perform almost any humiliating act in order to score a hit. However, dogs don't need food; they will do the same act for attention and the reward of a cuddle or even just a "Good boy". Children will also help just in order to get a smile, a cuddle, a "Good boy". It may, however, not be their best option. The role of performing seal, circus dog, or beautiful child is ideal for someone with an intellectual age of 2, like a seal, a dog or a 2-year old child. It ill becomes an adult.

Helping an asker by answering the question does not help the responder, and it rarely helps the asker. If the asker is a teacher, manager or police officer, then the relationship between the asker and the responder is clear. However, the situation is more complicated when the asker is a child, whose natural curiosity makes questions a natural act.

Facts are easily forgotten; what is valuable is the process of discovery. Pleasure in discovery motivates more discovery.

Easy satisfaction is like eating sugar; a drug that needs increasing quantities to reach the same hit.

In education, teachers and students. When do the students learn most, when the student asks the question or when the teacher asks the question ? When does the teacher learn the most, when he asks the question or when a student asks a question ? Learning is proportional to the time spent answering the question oneself.

In work, ready answers destroy creativity, prevent delegation and inhibit personal development. In social circles, answering questions stifles the mind. People who love pub quizzes use the answer to halt discussion and thought on all the other questions that one question raises.

In comedy, there is a straight and a funny guy. The funny guy steals the punchline by delivering the answer to a question; he also steals the limelight, the psychological lead. Often, the public is not aware of the straight man, dismissing him as "not as funny" as the funny man. [81] Both are necessary for comedy, both share the same sense of humour, but answering the question takes control.

Many comedians are not even prepared to share the limelight with their own straight guy. They perform both roles, asking the question and then answering it. Stand-up comedians specialise in this kind of humour.

---

[81] As in *The Telegraph*, "John Eric Bartholomew was the funny one and Ernie Wise the perfect example of a straight man." [175]

Confuse

*People can come up with statistics to prove anything,
Kent. 40% of all people know that.* [82]

Confusion is a tactic to win arguments with
false information, and can include the use of
ambiguous terms, abstract nouns, vague verbs, non-
sequiturs, spurious facts and personal insults.

Without a logical basis, any decisions made
through confusion are likely to be erroneous and
costly.

---

[82] Homer Simpson defending a shocking 900% increase in
heavy sack beatings. [176]

Habit

Behaviour

Sow confusion through the use of falsehoods, insults and verbal torrent to win arguments.

Roles

Confounder
Confounded

Outcomes

The confounder wins the argument. The confounded fails in his attempt to use politely logic and facts to reach a reasonable conclusion.

The confounder then avoids taking responsibility for his or her actions, while simultaneously blaming others for the outcomes. Progress is stifled.

Interpretation

The confounder wants to maintain independence or increase superiority, and sees the confounded as a threat.

Alternative behaviour

The confounded can refuse to listen to the confounder, and demand specific action or facts.

Identification

The easiest way to identify a confounder is by his use of 3rd party references, which can be academic tomes, gods, dead or isolated people, or spurious facts.

Obey

Humans are naturally obedient to figures of authority. In the Hofling hospital experiment, an unknown doctor successfully instructed nurses to give a double lethal dose. In the Milgram experiment, men in white coats told students to give actors a painful electric shock.

Authority bias in humans evolves from typical social mammalian behaviour, acquiescing to the decisions made by the alpha male and, in societies that are more complex, to those higher in the pecking order.

Obedience to instructions from government is overall beneficial, as long as tax rates overall remain reasonable, about 10%, while protection is provided to private business, and if some of the tax revenue is invested in improvement.

Habit

Behaviour

One person instructs another to behave in a certain way.

Roles

Commander
Complier

Outcomes

The commander gets one-up on the complier. The complier maintains his subservient position. Useful behaviour is reinforced, wasteful behaviour too.

Interpretation

The commander wants to claim, maintain or increase his superiority, and sees the complier as an opportunity.

Alternative behaviour

The complier can refuse to obey, usually eliciting a violent reaction.

Identification

The tax demand for homage, service and contribution, and mainly affects adult males interacting with non-kin adult males. Taxation is always costly, with only accidental, delayed and indirect benefits. Evasion is illegal and avoidance discouraged.

Taxation is a unique human behaviour which would be abnormal in any wild animal.

Obedience, on the other hand, affects all humans, not just adult males, and many other animals. It derives from normal social behaviour within a kin group. Obedience relates to specific commands, which can be immediately beneficial, reciprocal or costly. There is no obligation to obey, evasion and avoidance are permitted.

Children obey kin and non-kin, adults obey each other, and the outcomes can be immediately beneficial. For example, in a football team, a manager may enforce a tax relationship with the team members, but each team member, while carrying out his function, may instruct the other players; the goalkeeper forming the line, the free-kick, corner or throw-in taker instructing the forwards, the captain instructing the defence.

Believe

Belief is not behaviour, until someone says "I believe …"

By definition, beliefs are false, unproven or contradictory.

Stating belief has nothing to do with facts, and everything to do with group membership. It is the other people in the group that are interesting, not the object of belief.

Belief is often assumed, especially regarding the behaviour and motivation of others. This can appear as fundamental attribution error, or the dualism of good (pertaining to the believer) and evil (pertaining to the other person).

Those who believe in absurdities can also permit, pardon or perform atrocities. Ignorance, blind, copying, repetition and belief caused many of the historical atrocities.

Habit - Believe

Behaviour

State "I believe . . ."

Roles

Believer
God
Audience

Outcomes

The believer claims membership of a group.

Interpretation

The believer communicates his membership of a faith to an audience, either to find out the status (believer/disbeliever) of the other, to encourage membership for an unbeliever, or simply to position oneself in the ranks of a particular group.

Belief can be a justification (irrational excuse) for certain behaviour. The claim for belief may hide unexpressed reasons for that behaviour. The believer selects an appropriate belief that supports it to avoid having to discuss it.

Alternative behaviour

Doubt.

Empires of Decline

Countries, states and cities that tax heavily exist in a spiral of decline, from which it is difficult to escape. All problems stem from, or are exacerbated by, a high tax rate. The cash extracted from the economy reduces that available for investment in new businesses or in improvement, for social or health care, for protection against foreign invasion or pirates. Workers prefer employment in a government sinecure or protection through social security of unemployment insurance to the risk inherent in a hire-or-fire economy. Bankers prefer to loan money to those working for government or a government-sponsored monopoly.

Intelligence would encourage all those in government to reduce the high tax rate. However, this is not possible. Patronage is essential to maintain their positions in the government hierarchy; reducing tax rates would require reducing patronage. Instead, government members and civil servants find themselves demanding greater homage, greater loyalty, more service and contribution from their subordinates, including from the electorate, the citizens and the tax-payers. The psychological need for people used to adulation and sycophancy only increases at times of stress and criticism. Thus, when things are already bad, the government makes things worse.

There are exceptions. Some leaders do try to keep up with pre-election promises to reduce government expenditure and taxes. Some measures do show a temporary decline in government tax revenues, government borrowing or either measure relative to GDP, per capita GDP or per head of population. However, it is much easier to reduce tax rates, which paradoxically have the effect of increasing taxation. Although they also stimulate the economy, they usually hide stealth taxes and encourage playing with rates.

The major problem is that, even if tax revenues, rates and numbers of taxes fall, the governments expenses continue to rise. This necessitates increasing the triple-D of government, debt, debasement and default. [83]

The long-term trend is that the overall tax rate is rising, and the overall health of many countries is falling. This includes most of the so-called "western" nations. Some are doing better than others. The USA and the UK hide their disastrous position by heavy borrowing, thanks to the credit available from a free currency. European nations struggle with the stricter controls of their central bank, but survive on higher overt taxes. In both cases, the total national debts approximate to more than can ever be repaid by the current population. [84]

---

[83] This compares with the triple-A of government, acquire, ameliorate and amortise.

[84] Governments are canny enough to never say such a thing, or to permit such numbers from appearing in any official document.

The Rise of an Empire

All imperial decline follows a period of imperial growth.

The growth appears as economic growth but more importantly as population growth. When together, they produce a spiral of growth that seems both inevitable and permanent. Such a growth is often accompanied by increasing military capability (the equipment and manpower) and the capacity (the will to use it).

One outcome of population growth is emigration. This should be seen as a success, as long as it is due to the increasing population and population density in the home territory. Emigration, both temporary for economic reasons, and permanent for settlement, can co-operate with military adventures, another synergistic combination leading to a spiral of foreign imperialism.

The population growth inevitably leads at times to unemployment. This should be seen as a sign of success, at least potential success, for population stagnation and full employment inevitably kills economic growth.

The growth of population and economy are uncontrolled, and have little effect on external forces, the environment, climate, disease, and other nations' activities. Sometimes, external forces work in favour of continued growth. At other times, they brake that growth, and even throw it into reverse. When these interact, they result in a series of booms and busts.

Traditionally a vehicle for criticism of government, they are the best measure of its success. [85]

10% - Imperial Peak & the Warning Point

A reasonable rate of taxation is 10%. At this rate, individuals will continue their activities without significant changes. They will neither reduce production to avoid taxes, nor change their business methods to evade them. Whether the government is beneficial for the tax-payers depends on whether they invest in improvement or squander the revenue on luxury or war; however, this level of taxation at least provides an opportunity for success.

Given a nation's geology, geography and climate, and the current level of technology, its possibilities reach a peak at this level of taxation. In history, many nations achieve prominence much later in their tax cycles, as both military adventurism and artistic splendour, symptoms of social failure, are more popular and leave more cultural traces than economic and demographic success. [86]

---

[85] Unfortunately, the critics are tempted to push the government to intervene, an enthusiasm for disaster, which experience does nothing to diminish. Governments are not capable of creating the conditions for growth of either population or economy, neither do they control the weather, disease or their neighbours. Any intervention can only be costly and, at best, accidentally successful in achieving some minor victory.

[86] The so-called *Golden Age* usually comes in the century after this peak is reached, or even after entering terminal decline.

Overall tax rates above 10% are injurious, but their effects are often hidden by a greater investment in improvement, by neighbours with higher tax rates, and by financial shenanigans such as increased debt, debasement and default. The worst behaviour is simply the failure to accrue for future expenses, as long-term expenditure becomes an ever greater part of the government's budget. [87]

There is a great difference between humans and wild animals. The history of the human world is a history of great empires that rose and then, seemingly inevitably, collapsed, sometimes to see another empire rise on the ashes, at other times to disappear under the forces of nature and reappear as a mystery under the trowel of archaeologists. It is a millennial process.

Wild animal populations also fluctuate, often wildly, but these short-term fluctuations are correlated on the availability of food. Population has little correlation with pollution, population density, population growth rates or other factors which might be thought to affect their numbers.

---

[87] Most governments oblige businesses operating in their territories to accrue for all obligations, using the generally-accepted accounting principles (GAAP), which they steadfastly avoid in their own accounting. Government obligations include the salaries and pensions of all their current employees, the leases on government buildings, the maintenance of all its equipment, including military vehicles, planes and ships. Government debt is offset by government assets, which usually include huge tracts of land and could include even more through expropriation. However, this rarely includes any improved land, and unimproved land was inherited from the previous government. The net gain or loss of land (and resaleable assets in general) would be an interesting measure of government success.

On the other hand, populations of captive animals, usually well-fed, struggle to rise and often collapse. Bee colonies and pandas are two common examples. For animals in controlled societies, a surplus of food is insufficient to provide the motivation for life.

In John Calhoun's experiments with captive rats and mice, well-fed and protected rodents died out from the stifling conditions in which they were kept. The lack of freedom to group select, to mate, to act, encouraged by the extravagant supply of food, diminishes the drive to procreate, to raise and protect offspring.

Human empires, also, have little correlation with food supply, or with pollution, growth rates, population density, natural resources, climate, race, culture or education. On the contrary, the most attractive locations have an inverse correlation with pollution and natural resources, the great cities and the flood plains of major rivers. Only on retirement, when humans are no longer productive or reproductive, do they seek out the quiet rural pastures.

There is, however, massive correlation between relative population growth and the intervention of government. As government intervention in life rises from zero, its protection and investment provides a stimulus to the population, which increases. After reaching a certain point, however, government intervention is counter-productive, and the population declines relative to other territories.

The 10% is therefore both the point at which the economy and population are growing at the optimum rate, but also a warning, for any increase will see a reduction in that growth and an end to the spiral of success which it had driven.

As long as the natural circumstances allow, a nation at 10% tax can continue to grow, so fast that the government is not able to grow itself fast enough to increase the net tax take. This situation can continue for many years, even centuries.

Eventually, however, foreign intervention, population growth to the limits of the land available, changes in climate, or unanticipated technological developments can lead to a problem, where the government intervention increases faster than the economic growth, and where the effective tax take increases. This combination still reversible, but already presents greater challenges to implement changes in policy, reductions in government spending and reductions in taxation.

The most likely outcome, especially over the long term, is ever increasing government expenditure, increasing number of taxes, increasing tax rates, fewer and more costly exemptions. In response, there is greater avoidance (diminished production) and increased evasion (offshoring, trusts, crime).

Much of the government behaviour is hidden behind the rhetoric of democratic politics. Much of their intervention, especially tax increases, comes in the form of *solidarity*, or *welfare*, *social security*, *unemployment insurance*, at the behest of the vocal population, or at least of a part of it.

The government is not always to blame. As economies stagnate, individuals escalate their interpersonal conflicts for resolution by government agencies, the police, the law courts, and parliament. Governments rarely involve themselves in personal affairs except to extract taxes, and invitations such as these are welcomed, to everyone's loss, except the government. As well as personal conflict, governments can intervene at the request of associations, enterprises and between consumers and their suppliers, all to their detriment.

Businessmen and aristocrats can still negotiate exemptions, although these are now more expensive and provide fewer benefits. As taxes rise, there is an increasing tendency to avoid them through underproduction. Evasion is still not generally profitable, most criminals spend more time in jail than evading taxes.

Wars, plagues and environmental activism facilitate the job of government, leading to temporary and permanent increases in taxation, government obligations and loss of individual rights. The biggest loss is in that of personal responsibility, except when under prosecution. The abject following of standard rules diminishes the need for brains, leading to dysgenic fertility. Increasing numbers of laws infringe traditional freedoms, restrict them or remove them completely. Basic freedoms to assemble, to behave in ways that hurt no-one, to participate in consensual acts are proscribed.

Even so, however bad things may appear to be, nations with medium-level taxation may still be able to improve their situation, relatively to other nations, and absolutely. Tax factors affect economies and demographies over many years. A generation can be 25 years, and this period can change many things. Simple or accidental changes which lead to rapid population growth, technological advance and economic growth can reduce declared and actual debt, relative government expenditure and overall tax rates.

Government reactions are to increase their attacks on the vulnerable, but also to attack those with the most money. How they select the victims for the next tax rises, exile, or extermination is standard throughout the global tax economy.

1.   Identification – naming allows classification as an enemy, as well as *them*, as opposed to *us*.
2.   Symbolisation – forced wearing of labels, clothes, masks to facilitate their identification.
3.   Demonization – assignation of crime, theft, treason, economic profiteering, pollution, or disgusting habits – smell, diet, religion, hygiene habits.
4.   Organisation – takes time, money, people
5.   Communication - through media propaganda,
6.   Polarisation – escalation of aggression, hatred and violence (simplified by 1 & 2) forces people to take sides or acquiesce in the battle. Those who do nothing are part of the problem.
7.   Separation – isolation of the enemy facilitates whatever extraction will take place.
8.   Obligatory service, forced labour, incarceration (removal from the gene pool), sterilisation, extermination – not murder, execution or killing, but extermination like a pest.
9.   Denial [88]

---

[88] Lifted by, but modified, from Genocide Watch, as quoted by Jan Danzig investigative journalist.

The Tipping point - 50%

Economies enter a terminal decline with tax rates of 50%.

When tax rates reach 50%, perhaps divided up into federal, state and local corporate, income and sales taxes, obligatory contributions for solidarity, unemployment and retirement insurance, additional taxes on tobacco, alcohol, energy and cars, import and export tariffs, legal fines for communal law breaking, penalties and congestion charges, military or civil service, half the population is working directly for the government, producing nothing, while the rest is working to pay for them. [89] The latter's motivation is simply to join the government in any capacity, and to transfer all wealth, produce and labour to a tax haven.

No economy can thrive with such high tax rates as 50%, and the evidence is easily visible in countries such as those of the old Soviet Union, the old communist bloc, and modern western Europe. Tax rates are high, avoidance is rife and evasion is the only way to make money. The only businesses that thrive are those with powerful lobby groups, granted exemptions and public funding, charities (a euphemism for tax evasion) and personal trusts (another euphemism for evasion).

It's not surprising that billionaires like Donald Trump prefer to play politics. Billionaires like Bill Gates prefer to run a tax-free charity. Jeff Bezos

---

[89] Wartime conscription almost always leads to a 50% tax rate, as not only is the male population providing service, but the economy is also entirely focused on the war effort.

manages a global business, where most of the profit is accounted for in low-tax states. The alternative is to work really hard, and then see 30%, 40% or 50% of their earnings taken away. At the other end of the scale, the workers see their wage packets diminish, or the cost of living increase. The lucky ones keep their jobs. Government attempts at intervention may lead to hyperinflation, shortages or famine.

Apart from federal or national corporation tax, the tax take also includes state and local taxes, payroll or national insurance contributions by the employer, and income taxes and insurance contributions by the employee. All these taxes come essentially from the industrial investor. Any business has to buy raw materials, commodities or consumables, and these are also taxed, and their suppliers suffer the same taxation on profits, employment, consumption and production. The opportunity for profiteering with so many taking a profit are therefore restricted.

With government inherently unprofitable and controlling half the national economy, the nation can only fail compared to nations with much less intervention. Debt can only grow. Taxes need to increase, either new taxes or increased rates, or conquest of new tax territories with new tax-payers. Economic problems encourage domestic and international strife. Wars generally increase debt and taxation further. The economy declines, the population declines.

Much of this decline is still invisible to those who do not want to see it, who use the wrong measures of wealth and growth, or who look at short-term measures. Society does not change, for the pernicious government intervention may have been justified or ignored, but the level increases to the point where it affects the behaviour of the majority. Freedoms are the exception, and resistance is avoided as likely to lead to unendurable trouble. Even to step out of the house requires an identity card, a permit, am excuse backed up by an authority, with limited time, or geography. Citizens are nothing more than feudal vassals, owned by their government for the sole purpose of paying them homage, service and contribution.

The collapse of the Roman Empire did not mean the death of every individual in a single, momentous cataclysm. Rome was not built in a day, nor did it die in a day. There was a long, slow process of evolution which culminated in the rise of the Christian empires and the Ottoman. We now know that much of the decline in the western Empire after 400AD was caused by climate change, a massive cooling caused by natural factors, or perhaps by a reduction in Roman industrial production if one believes modern climate change ideas.

However, the Roman state reached its peak in the year Jesus Christ was born, not four hundred years later. It peaked as taxes reached a critical point, the point beyond which it was more profitable for entrepreneurs to seek government jobs than to invest in industry, trade, farming, or any of the productive tasks that provide essential or even luxury goods. The long decline of the Empire lasted fifteen hundred years. When exactly it went from the peak under Octavian to a collapse is an academic argument.

The effect of the economy on the population is also pernicious but invisible to close observers. There is a decline in the indigenous population. They have fewer children, later, and more of them emigrate.

Meanwhile, the obvious signs are increased immigration. Whereas in the period of imperial growth, immigrants swept the streets and drove the buses, in decline they are the bankers and merchants keeping the government afloat. They provide the mercenaries protecting the leadership from their own electorate and from foreign enemies. They are soon the conquerors.

Women increasingly take power. While they are fully occupied during the years of growth, a declining population permits them to use their superior communication and political skills to climb the male hierarchical ladders in trade and government.

Individuals leave the taxed economy and operate partly or exclusively in the subsistence economy.

Conquest by immigration is inevitable, but civil war and conquest by foreign powers are possible scenarios. Any idea that "it could never happen here" needs immediate disabusing; Persia, China and India were powerful, if not the most powerful nations in their time, and all were conquered by small forces from a little island in the North Sea. All the United States' military might, nuclear arsenal and aircraft carriers failed to prevent the physical occupation of dozens of city centres in 2020 and even of the Capitol in early 2021. Britain, bankrupt and at war with Germany, was invaded by American troops in 1943, and they have still not left. The Roman Empire was partly conquered by Germans, partly by Arabs and then another partly by Turks.

The Terminal Economy

It is worth looking at the worst economy in the world to understand what is possible and where the world is going. The country with the worst economy in the world is the United States.

Economic growth stems from natural resources and relative costs. The United States of America is one of the countries with the richest natural resources, even if many of them have been exploited for hundreds of years. It is still a much larger country than all but three others. It should, therefore, have a strong economy based on natural resources. However, since the Second World War it has increased its tax rate.

Although the notional sales, income and corporate taxes are relatively low compared to European countries, the United States is the world's biggest debtor. This means of avoiding taxation is still a tax, on both the population of tax-payers and the economy. Money borrowed by the government to fund its vanity projects and buying votes is removed from the economy. It is no longer available to provide cheap credit to build factories, improve infrastructure

While US wages average about $30,000, the official national debt of $28 Trillion works out at about $85,000. However, only 43% of Americans are net tax-payers, so these will pay $196,000 each. The real tax rate of the US is therefore over 600%.

These numbers are only for the official debt. The US government refuses to accrue for obligatory future expenses. This includes an additional $21 Trillion for social security, $33 Trillion for Medicare, and future pay and pensions for government employees.

The total US debt, if calculated according to GAAP in the way in which the US government forces private corporations to account, would surpass $162 Trillion, or $491,000 per person, or $1.1 Million per tax-payer. [90] This gives an effective tax rate of 3000%.

Against this debt of tens or a hundred trillion dollars, the US Federal Reserve holds assets worth $144 Billion. This includes all the gold and foreign currency which is the only liquid asset. Government property, land, is probably worth $2 Trillion. Government expenditure to create the debt has created little that is saleable. Even to the total land value of the United States is only $23 Trillion, about the same as the official debt. [91]

To hide the scale of the problem, the Federal Reserve holds $8 Trillion of government debt, which it lists as an asset. In other words, the government owes the Fed $8 Trillion, and has left an IOU in the Fed safe. Separating the Federal Reserve from the US Government thus makes an $8 Trillion debt disappear and become an asset somewhere else. In reality, it is just a debt.

In order to pay off the total national debt, if it remained at $162 Trillion, the living tax-payers would have to work for 37 years paying tax at 100%. In reality, the current workforce is already incapable of paying the debt. Realistically, it would take at least three generations to pay down the debt.

---

[90] The US Debt Clock provides interesting data sourced from the US Government. [189]

[91] According to William D. Larson from the USA Bureau of Economic Analysis in a paper published in 2015 based on numbers from 2009. [188]

However, the debt is not stagnant, and continues to grow. Current plans for COVID merely ensure that the growth will accelerate. Meanwhile, other costs rise and revenues shrink with the collapsing economy.

The US government, or more accurately the Federal Reserve System, is already printing money, which it euphemises into quantitative easing. The development of fractional reserve banking allows any bank to lend more money than it possesses. It is a giant Ponzi scheme that has frequently led to bank crashes, whenever the depositors worry about their money and try to withdraw it. The only way to stop the panic is to close the bank doors, which usually increases the panic, or to guarantee the deposits. The Fed was set up to provide this guarantee; it is just an even bigger Ponzi scheme.

Normally, the central banks like the Fed limit the amount of money that a local bank can lend. The fraction of its deposits can change, but it usually needs to keep at least 10% or 20% of its deposits in reserve for emergencies and to prevent runs in times of panic. However, after the worsening economic situation and the COVID panic, the Fed has reduced this level of protection to 0%. If there is a run on American banks now, there is no reserve to turn to.

Historically, printing money stimulates inflation, which reduces the value of the debt, as well as of savings. It is a stealth tax on the rich. However, in the 21st Century, with low levels of interest rates and inflation, printing money merely keeps the inflation above 0%. Without it, prices would already have collapsed, as it is only the ever-increasing debt that permits people to buy at the inflated prices. If anything, prices are even more inflated in Europe and Japan, but the US also maintains prices artificially high, especially in food commodities like sugar.

There are more millionaires in the US than there are unemployed. The proliferation of wealthy individuals is part of the American Dream, but it also makes them a natural target for those who talk about *solidarity*, *equality* and *social justice*.

These words are euphemisms for taking money and confiscating property from the rich. This is akin to a sugar baby taking money and stuff from her sugar daddy. This form of prostitution is common among those with no qualifications looking for easy money to satisfy an addiction. However, the problem is the addiction, not the funds. Once the money is spent, the addiction remains.

There is an easier way than taxation to achieve the same result, and that is the decriminalisation of theft. Those with the most wealth will quickly find that those with the least will take it from them. This Robin Hood act would result in the fast rebalancing of wealth. It would require no administration cost, no permanent drain on the economy or the state in the form of pensions, and would find a natural equilibrium which would be impossible otherwise.

No socialist suggests this, because the last thing that a socialist government wants is to hand control of wealth redistribution to the private citizen, even when this is the most effective way of doing things. Most socialists who suggest taxing the rich are themselves rich, but as they are government employees, their salaries are in many case just tax receipts. The more taxes they collect, the more they can pay themselves, and the greater the benefits they accrue by offering patronage and pork barrels.

The other reason that governments don't do this is because they also know that it simply wouldn't work. Rich people don't keep their wealth in liquid assets. Their wealth is mainly made up of stocks and gilts, property, yachts, and memberships. Poor people cannot eat these things. They may be able to sell the wife's jewellery and son's sports car, a few watches and works of art, but never the kind of billions or trillions of dollars that are needed. This reality is obvious to anyone involved in crime, but seemingly ignored by politicians.

A simpler way to achieve the same result is simply to print money. A government that prints its own money can pay all its debts and expenses, including its wage bill. It does not need to balance its books. The inflation caused by the printing will reduce the value of any liquid assets, savings, held by rich people. Inflation will also affect industry, again hitting those richest whose wealth is held in stocks and shares.

The ultimate goal would be to dispense with industry completely, simply printing money to buy all a country's needs from its neighbours. As long as the neighbours are prepared to accept the printed money, everything should be alright.

The only problem with this popular theory is that it doesn't work, otherwise everybody would be doing it. The cryptocurrency industry would not have bothered with the complex and expensive process of mining bitcoins and etheriums if they could simply open a bank and print money.

The simple way to debunk any economic theory, such as buying a lottery ticket, is simply take it to the extreme. If it is worth buying one lottery ticket, then it is surely better still to buy all the lottery tickets. If it is worth betting on one number on roulette, then it must be better to bet on all of them. The result of such *reductio ad absurdam* is always absurd, the cost of lottery tickets or gambling on roulette always exceeds the winning prizes.

Those who propose the magic money tree are perhaps oblivious to the extreme example. Instead of working, everybody can just sit at home and print money from their computer. If the government insists that all such paper money is legal tender, then there should be no problem. The nation would struggle to import, and there would be no food, fuel or shelter, but it would solve the problem of debt.

Those who propose to endlessly increase national debt, do not propose to stop collecting taxes. If printing money had no negative effect on the economy, and there really was no limit on the amount that could be printed, then printing a little bit more to cover current tax revenues would have no negative effect. This would be the one proof that they actually believed what they said, yet they do not do it. Clearly, at some point, tax receipts will be needed, and tax-payers need to be kept accustomed to the process. The magic money tree, like the goose that lays golden eggs, will one day get the chop, and then the only source of revenue for the government will be taxes.

Unfortunately, it is unlikely that any government will resist the public pressure to increase spending. Individuals may try to reduce spending, and they may achieve some successes, but the overall rate will continue to rise. Governments can continue to borrow money until they run out of lenders due to war or economic collapse. Then they can continue to print money, but will struggle to pay for its imports, and the local supply of essentials will fail. Finally, it will suffer the inevitable civil strife. Foreign mercenaries, originally engaged to defend the millionaires and the pensioners, will take over the country. The national debt will be wiped clean, and the process will start again.

Totalitarianism

Foreign conquest by immigration or military action may avoid the worst alternative, or may invite it. A totalitarian state involves the total loss of privilege, freedom and rights for the original inhabitants. This is usually justified by a need to protect the immigrants, who now control the country, its politics, trade, economy, taxation, and military, but it has also arisen from benevolent desires to improve the situation for the indigenous population. In the heydays of totalitarianism, neither national socialism nor international communism succeeded in achieving their objectives. However, they both have powerful support in the 21st Century, and it is only a matter of time before their attractions result in national power.

The worst form of totalitarianism occurs with foreign leadership. The changes grant the foreigners extra-territorial powers, while preventing the natives from prosecuting them. This facilitates the foreign exploitation, further increasing their inroads. Natives are punished increasingly heavily for crimes against the foreigners, especially for rebellion.

Even without leaving their house, there are a wide range of offences that citizens can commit, and for which little evidence is needed for conviction other than accusation and inevitable media pressure. Outside, they face an endless array of forces, rules and regulations and punishments.

To legal infringements are added those invented by the forces of law and order, by executive agencies and by the court system, even including the juries that almost always fail to support the citizen and instead support the forces of oppression. Foreigners add their own inexplicable rules to the oppression.

Civil war is a possible scenario, although not one that usually results in improvements for the tax-payer and citizen. Wars destroy infrastructure, kill, and leave a pile of debt which only the local tax-payer will cover. The victor will also add the additional policing costs and reparations to the bill. The empire will collapse even faster.

Sleep

The end result is difficult to imagine for an existing country, but easy to see in the many examples of history.

The classic lost empire is the Maya, whose pyramids and temples nature covered so that it took hundreds of years for Europeans to discover just how great it had been.

The Maya were the most civilised of the pre-Columbian American societies. Yet their collapse was just as certain as that of those the Spanish encountered when they reached the American mainland. Without any obvious external threat, the Maya destroyed themselves, abandoned their cities and retreated to the remotest rural areas. For two hundred years, warlords operated in the power vacuum, providing some interest for historians and gossips, but doing nothing to resurrect the culture. The Spanish conquered the Mayan lands and introduced a foreign culture. The Maya kept their calendar, their diet and the subsistence lifestyle, but suffered the oppression expected from a foreigner.

There are many other examples, although few that really disappeared. The Chinese and Indian empires surprised their conquerors by the ease with which they fell, although their conquerors perhaps ignored the hundreds of years that their predecessors had failed to do the same thing. The Roman Empire was sacked by Vandals and Goths, a feat still unexplained by fans of the Legions and their invincible reputation. [92]

Whatever new empires grow in the geographical zone of an old one, they will be different from the old ones. Created on a different tax structure, with different governments, different opportunities for patronage, and different tax-payers. They may carry the same name, speak the same language and follow the same religion, but it will be a different empire. Rome was a very

---

[92] The Legions had defeated the Macedonians, who had defeated the Thebans, who had defeated the Spartans who had defeated the Athenians who had defeated the Persians.

different empire under catholic popes than it was under pagan emperors.

Conclusion

Europe reached the tipping point in 2020. The USA and the UK are near to it. The recent behaviour of the population in all three is likely to push them down the terminal decline. The future is a relative loss of competitive, economic and demographic power. Europe is closest to the abyss, the US farthest, but all are already on the slippery, downward slope.

There is little that anyone can do to prevent this, and even less likelihood that anyone will. Evolution may yet produce a solution, but most of human history shows a monotonous repetition of societal failure, and there is nothing about 2020 that signals any difference this time.

Other nations will take advantage of the decline. There may be a great empire to replace the western, European, culture, although previous history shows that chaos provides the link in the chain of imperial power.

Intelligence

The popular theory that humans evolved greater intelligence than other animals and used it to outperform them, demographically and geographically, is popular but incorrect or, at least, incomplete. Intelligence is a *sine qua non*, but there is no evidence that the great advances were achieved uniquely by intelligence. Other animals with less intelligence reached similar ranges of expansion and prolificy. Earlier human species with smaller intelligence covered similar ranges.

As the western world enters its golden age, the great works of its intelligence, the libraries, the museums, and the theatres are closed. Intelligent men and women have closed them, for reasons that make no sense at all. Closure will only exacerbate the terminal economic problems faced by these nations. By the time that COVID is history, along with Brexit and Trump, people will wonder how intelligent people can panic so.

Meanwhile, the rest of the human world has been getting on with what unintelligent animals do best, eat, sleep, defecate and mate. Perhaps this is the true sign of intelligence. At a species level, at a nation level, in terms of imperial history, the only intelligent measure of a people's intelligence is the number of offspring carrying their genes.

In 2020, only a few members of government in a few countries managed to implement plans that were the result of intelligent decision making. All the rest, including all the western nations, implemented plans that were obviously and immediately flawed, and that after a year were still obviously flawed.

Role of government

Humans provide ample evidence that their intelligence is not the primary factor in their great numbers or their global expansion. They use their great brain not to find new ways to increase the population of the planet, but for politicking, to get one-up on their neighbours and stay there. No greater waste is seen than in politics itself, a house of shifty liars, profiteers and snake-oil salesmen who bankrupt their country. The year 2020 has shown the behaviour of governments and the media, and the public who in the main support them, or at least acquiesce to such behaviour.

Brexit, COVID and the United States election year will remain important subjects of debate for many years, due to their long-term effects. Global government debt has doubled in a year, and long-term accrued obligations have massively increased. In spite of all the government action, there has been no discernible effect on the major problems that governments claimed they were dealing with. Britain remains tied to Europe by hundreds of legal, diplomatic and military agreements. The United States still receives the majority of its essential population growth from immigration, and its status in global diplomacy is at an all-time low. COVID is now endemic in all countries except Australia, New Zealand, Taiwan and Singapore, whose populations will remain incarcerated on their island kingdoms forever, or until future governments find face-saving ways of releasing them.

Members of government justify their behaviour using their propaganda, policy documents, political theories, and euphemisms. They use nouns, especially abstract nouns, and adjectival nouns to define their behaviour, which is now converted into caring, providing for a fairer, more just, society. In reality, it is just an excuse for tax-collectors to demand homage, service and a financial contribution, from which they will get a psychological benefit, a new swimming pool and a cut for their Cayman Islands bank account.

Governments were essential for the creation of the European empires. However, government is much less about governing than about tax collection and the disbursement of these funds.

At the individual level, members of government are interested in their personal promotion, in both senses of the word. Keeping their job comes second. Worries about the electorate, the population at large, ethics or morality, come far behind if at all. There is nothing sinister nor immoral in this; it is no different than the behaviour of everyone else on the planet.

Role of people

Those who don't want to climb the greasy pole of politics, squander their intelligence on work, ritual and hobbies. When confronted by a member of government demanding homage, compliance with a new law, service or contribution, the most common reaction is acquiescence.

As individuals, humans behave in an intelligent manner, selecting the course of action that promises the greatest benefit. The most important benefit is the freedom to procreate, but others include the freedom to work. Acquiescence usually provides the greatest benefits, even if it also incurs the obligation to pay taxes.

In reality, the courses available are limited by geography, history and other individuals, as well as by the physiology and psychology of the individual, all of which are interdependent and which change over time. The human intelligence is such that this subordination is rationalised into the decision-making process, or simply absorbed into the subconscious.

The most typical characteristic of human beings is this self-delusion. Intelligence is an attractive trait to possess, and it is easy for an individual to compare itself with other animals. These chew cud, defecate on their food, and are eaten by lions. Compared to these lesser beings, humans are indeed intelligent. They chew salad, defecate inside their homes, and are eaten by worms.

In spite of the evidence that governments were incapable of governing wisely, and that oppositions were supporting governments or proposing equally faulty policies, electorates continued to vote for the system of government.

Taxation is the answer

The only human behaviour that correlates with massive population growth, as well as with imperial decline, is taxation. Taxation is the interaction between non-kin adult humans, especially males. One or other, sometimes both, sometimes neither, will demand homage from the other, the right to later demand service and contribution. The other must fight or acquiesce, avoid or evade. In return for homage, the tax-collector makes or the tax-payer assumes an ephemeral promise of taxation.

Once the promise of protection is in place, citizens can invest in improvement. They know who the government is, what its rate of taxes is on the property being improved, and they can calculate the economics of their business venture. They know that the government's interest in the success of the venture is such that they will defend it from bandits, pirates and other governments who want to take it over. The government will also protect them from unfair competition, those who don't pay their fair share of taxes, by taxing them, destroying their property or, if they are abroad, by implementing punitive import duties.

Once the relationship between government and citizen is established, many unknown individuals can co-operate, jointly investing time, effort and resources in common projects. Large teams of otherwise antagonistic adults and adolescents improve their environment, increasing its production for everyone's benefit. Governments themselves use the money that they collect to improve communications in their territory. The benefits accrue not just to the local population, but to their neighbours and the entire species as their behaviour is copied and repeated.

As tax societies become more complicated, at national levels, the governments operate oppressive systems. They are financially incompetent or, at best, disinterested. They generally increase their expenses, increasing tax rates and borrowings. Citizens evade by moving offshore or turning to crime, and avoid investing in taxable industries. The remaining tax-payers suffer increasing tax rates. Eventually, the only interesting work is that of the government, and nobody produces. The country is in decline.

A country whose economy is in decline will find that its population follows that decline. A lower rate of population growth than its neighbours, and especially a lower rate of organic growth, will inevitably result in increasing immigration, foreign investment, and the eventual takeover of the most important government positions by immigrants and foreigners.

Two million years of evolution have not changed the source of human behaviour, which is entirely controlled by genetic programming, proteins, parasites, pheromones and peer pressure.

The only way that the behaviour of the human species can be at the same time responsible for its great successes and for its stunning declines, regardless of the environment is for it to be the result of autonomic functions driven by genes and interactions, not by the environment. Human population has fluctuated historically due to the plague or warfare or environmental factors like volcanic eruptions affecting the climate. However, the population rises rapidly when the natural threat is passed. Human empires, however, decline and never recover. Sometimes they just disappear, Maya-like, covered in jungle foliage, to be discovered by surprised archaeologists. Others are conquered, like the Aztecs, by more aggressive, populous neighbours who can spare the numbers necessary for mass emigration or the money for a military invasion.

In 2020, government ministers, health advisors, members of the WHO, doctors, nurses, journalists, all demanded homage from the public. The one thing that they all wanted, was for individual members of the public to carry out a pointless, even dangerous, task to show their piety. Wearing a mask was the most popular show of homage, although staying indoors, remaining alone, working from home, and not enjoying oneself were other popular methods.

Government finance has advanced so far that taxes are no longer the immediate and essential ingredient. Human evolution may yet catch up and develop an allele that avoids the demands for service and contribution.

What can we do ?

As empires, the United Kingdom, the United States of America and the European Union are in terminal decline. However, this does not mean that the individuals inhabiting these territories should worry.

The decline is a slow process that can take several generations. It has already lasted more than a hundred years for Europe and Britain, since its peak in 1910, and before their populations decided they preferred fighting each other than growing their economies.

This also suggests the answer. People rarely enjoy what they think is good for them. Peace, growth, hard work and careful saving are never as much fun as wanton destruction, excitement, the raw emotion of fighting and the chance of meeting the new.

Conclusion

For an individual, the choice lies between maximising the benefits of the chaotic situation to increase wealth relative to those who fail to adapt, and deciding that the situation is not favourable and turning to war. War itself brings many opportunities for the survivors.

One option is no longer possible. For a thousand years, Europeans have emigrated, seeking fame, fortune or escape. The opportunity for Europeans is now reduced to emigration to the former European-dominated colonies of Canada, the USA, Australia and New Zealand. [93] While COVID restrictions abound, emigration is curtailed, but even when these are relaxed, the conditions for entry are not. Enthusiasm and English-language skills are no longer enough. Only the educated, experienced in sought after technologies need apply.

In the meantime, tax-payers should strive to pay as few as possible. They can grow their own food to avoid VAT, and recycle their own goods, to avoid more and to avoid the drain on their country's silver reserves. They can work off-grid, form cooperatives, or communities.

One thing not to do is to riot in the streets. That should be left to those who have nothing to lose and nothing to gain. There are two golden rules, show respect to the police, and never fight city hall. Any such action can only lead to greater expenditure and higher taxes, and a more rapid decline. Apart from those

---

[93] For the rich, residency and a passport are available for a price. Mexico, Panama,

offering services to the forces of law and order, it is a recipe for disaster.

The only real solution to the problem is to implement a system where only net tax-payers play at government. A proportional system, where the larger tax-payers have the greatest say, and the largest is the prime minister, has always worked in the past. Britain, the US and the European powers all developed their great empires in that way. They all lost their empires by encouraging the franchise among those who paid no taxes or who were net tax recipients.

It remains to be seen whether a period of dictatorship might place a benevolent and interested leader in a position of power, of just an accidental despot, that might yet reverse the course of European history.

Epilogue

Far more than a pandemic, 2020 was a year about panic. Government ministers panicked about Brexit, about the COVID death spiral and hospitals overflowing with patients, about race riots and police brutality, immigration and massive unemployment. The media encouraged the panic, and the public, mostly, added to it. It was truly a disaster for the human race, one which will remain as important for this century as the world wars of the last century.

As individuals, however, we should not worry about the fate of our species, or of the great civilisations in which we live. We have neither responsibility nor investment in it as a whole, only for our tiny part of it. We should only be interested in our own genes and our own behaviour.

Species survive for hundreds of thousands of years, individual humans at best a hundred. We should seek to enjoy in our own way the possibilities of life without fretting about the myriad problems that can potentially affect the species. Most of these problems are invented, inflated and communicated by individuals trying to justify their own sad lives by ruining yours.

There is no need to panic, and certainly no benefit from doing so. Panic stems from the mammalian instinct of fight/flight/freeze, which in human society is detrimental.

Don't give the panic mongers satisfaction. Avoid them if you can. If you can't, attack every one of their negative emotions with a positive one of your own. Enjoy sleep, enjoy breakfast, enjoy fresh air and exercise, enjoy the splash of cold water on your face, enjoy and share good food, enjoy the gentle touch of human companionship or that of animals, enjoy the pleasure of learning, of remembering, take the time to read a good book, or write a bad one, enjoy a laugh, a giggle, a fall, success in a venture and failure in many, a day lived, and the next day that promises so much.

Death is inevitable. It may come sooner, or it may come later; whenever it does come, it is better to regret it than to welcome it.

Appendices

It is not the purpose of this book to show that the behaviour of governments and their electorate in the years leading up to 2020, and during that momentous year, led to the implementation of policies that were detrimental to, even disastrous for, the economy, health and quality of life of the population. Others will do a more detailed, academic or popular job than this author. Some will attack the policies and the motivations or competence of those they perceive responsible. Equally, others will provide a robust defence based on emotional or even intellectual precepts. However, it is worth summarising the case for each of the three major issues mentioned in this book, and the major problem with the western approach for each one.

COVID-19

Experience has shown that communities faced with epidemics or other adverse events respond best and with the least anxiety when the normal social functioning of the community is least disrupted [94]

Government Intervention in Medicine

COVID-19 is a minor ailment, and was always going to be one. Millions of people die every year, and from chronic and acute illnesses that are far more infectious, painful and drawn out than COVID, whose treatment is far more difficult, dangerous for the professionals, and less successful. If governments are prepared to intervene, whatever the cost, in the case of a minor ailment, why have they not already done so in the case of the many more fatal diseases, why should they ever stop intervening for COVID, and why should they not immediately start interventions for every other equally serious medical problem ?

Respiratory Infections

Scientists have searched for a cure for the common cold for many years, and failed. In Britain, the exercise was led from the Common Cold Unit, just

---

[94] Dr. Donald Henderson, Presidential Medal of Freedom winner, eradicator of smallpox, recommending NOT to use social controls to limit the spread of infectious diseases.

outside Salisbury. Although in 45 years of trying, the British scientists never found a cure, they did identify and name the first coronaviruses, and developed the techniques for studying and growing them in the laboratory.

Colds are caused by different viruses, mainly rhinoviruses, 4 different human coronaviruses (about 15%) and certain influenza viruses.

Three human coronaviruses that cause the much more serious respiratory syndrome that gives SARS its name infect simultaneously the upper respiratory tract (mainly the nose, but also the throat, pharynx and upper larynx) and the lower respiratory tract (lower larynx, trachea, bronchi, alveolar ducts and alveoli in the lungs). Viruses and bacteria favour either one or the other. Infections of the upper respiratory tract may lead to infections of the lower tract, often by a different virus or bacterium.

Infections of the lower respiratory tract can be serious. Acute bronchitis, infection of the bronchi and trachea is rarely dangerous in itself, and is usually co-morbid with smoking, mining or air pollution. Whereas bronchitis affects the bronchi, and their inflammation reduces the ability of the lungs to take in air, pneumonia is an infection of the alveoli, and their inflammation reduces their ability to exchange oxygen for carbon dioxide in the blood stream. The much smaller size of the alveoli mean that infection is also more unpleasant, leading to a drowning feeling. Pneumonia can be fatal, as there is little direct treatment to cure it. Most treatment involves relieving symptoms, preventing secondary infections or damage from blood clots, for example, and the facilitation of respiration by providing oxygen – to increase the percentage of oxygen to make up for the reduced airflow, or to improve breathing by reducing

Symptoms and signs of lower respiratory tract infection are caused by the agent itself, damaging or even killing infected epithelial cells, but also by the body's own immune system, flooding the lungs with mucus in an attempt to clean them out by coughing.

COVID-19

COVID-19 is just the latest coronavirus to appear. It is a dangerous, infectious disease. Unlike the common cold coronaviruses, it leads to lower respiratory tract infections that, when co-morbid with other respiratory tract or immune problems, cause serious illness and even death.

However, it is not more dangerous than many other infectious diseases, such as tuberculosis, which kills millions of people worldwide, every year. Infectious respiratory diseases kill a million people every year without any government measures aimed at the mass population. Infectious intestinal diseases, like cholera, kill another million, again without any panic or mass measures.

As well as acute illnesses, chronic illnesses are killers, by far the greatest killers in the western world. Smoking, eating red meat, sugars and starches, or drinking alcohol are legal lifestyle choices that lead to a wide variety of disease. Lung cancer, mainly caused by smoking and air pollution, kills 1.75 million a year.

Cancer of the colon kills ¾ million, often caused by the combination of a rich diet and lack of exercise.

Cardiovascular diseases, including diabetes and obesity, are responsible for the greatest number of deaths, killing twenty million people a year, twenty times more than COVID. Governments could have imposed drastic restrictions on smoking and eating sugar, as well as forcing people outside to take exercise, which would have provided a massive boost to longevity and health. Instead they ignored the problem.

Improved longevity has introduced a range of morbidities which are responsible for the greatest number of life termination. Governments made no efforts during 2020 to manage the problem, instead isolating dementia patients, introducing severe restrictions on their care, and incarcerating them with infected COVID patients. Death rates from dementia in Britain and the USA soared, far in excess of recent averages and above the death rate for COVID.

Any government measures to control these other diseases and behaviours have not led to the mass restriction of freedoms, or the destruction of the global economy. Malaria used to kill millions of people every year, but government controls throughout the world have led to its eradication in many parts and, even in Africa, the number of deaths has dropped by half in the last twenty years, without any major social changes. Diarrhoeal diseases have also been controlled and reduced, although not, perhaps, by as much as a half, but at least by a half in the number of children under 5. [95]

---

[95] [180]

In 1947, 23,000 Britons died from tuberculosis, and 52,000 were newly infected. Fifty thousand children suffered from diphtheria, in the last year before widespread vaccination. The last great polio epidemic saw 7,000 cases and 500 deaths. All these diseases have been eradicated from Britain without major intervention in public behaviour, and as a standard part of childhood healthcare.

Smallpox in Britain was a relatively rare disease, with only 78 new cases and 15 deaths. Its eradication in Britain, India and elsewhere was carried out without any mass restrictions, focused only on those infected, their likely contacts, and the vulnerable individuals who could come into contact with the disease.

However, acute infectious diseases are not the major killers, 7 million a year die from polluted air, mostly from industries and transport regulated by governments. [96] Every year, close to two million people a year die from violence, half by their own hands, and about 300,000 at the hands of governments and other organisations, with weapons produced and sold with government approval, and at elections, with the approval of their electorate. [97]

COVID-19 is therefore neither the most important health concern, the most dangerous, nor the one most easily managed to produce a cost-effective, or even a successful result.

A few countries, some with good experience in dealing with pandemics, others by luck, have managed

---

[96] [179]

[97] All major weapon producing nations hold democratic, one person, one vote elections.

the COVID panic without destroying their economy and social life. Research into coronavirus shows that the best prevention comes from poor countries that are forced to consider economic issues, from countries with multiple endemic infectious diseases who are used to implementing containment practices in a cost-effective way and without endangering health workers.

Most European and western countries, however, have implemented severe lockdowns, obliged the wearing of masks, closed schools, shops, services, introduced curfews, travel permits, and enforced these measures with punitive police action. Many government measures to deal with COVID-19 have been arbitrary, unscientific and frequently contradictory to their own pronouncements.

The problem for governments is that they are poor structures for implementing medical controls. Given that banning tobacco or sugar would lose them the next election, governments are reduced to implementing measures that can have no hope of succeeding , but which carry some measure of public support, especially if the fear factor is wound up to fever pitch.

Pandemic

The pandemic started in warm countries (10°C is ideal, compared to 11-15°C ideal temperature for maximum human development) with high levels of sunlight (Iran, Italy, Spain and all the world after airplanes stopped flying and cars stopped moving), in humid, densely populated areas.

Correlated with high coronavirus mortality is a high life expectancy, which is self-evident because there are a lot more vulnerable old people to suffer from diseases that affect older people, but also obesity and lack of exercise, wealth as measured by GDP. Most victims have multiple morbidities, usually at least 3, with old age, diabetes and obesity being the holy trinity of COVID death statistics.

No attempt has been made by any government to reduce the age of this vulnerable cohort, to restrict their access to sugars, or to increase their exercise regimes. Most government interventions have led to increases in fast food intake, due to the closure of slow food outlets and the ban on social gatherings like family meal times, and restrictions on exercise due to the bans on team sports, school closures, public gatherings. [98] The cytokine storms stimulated by COVID infections are exacerbated by poor diet, especially a lack of vitamin B and magnesium. This is a typical result of lockdowns, with their interruptions to food distribution, the closure of restaurants, the ban on visiting friends and family, and a lack of travel.

There is one other correlation that is even more important for COVID mortality, and that is a high but declining life expectancy, such as exists in the GB and the USA, presumably because there is already a poor healthcare system aimed at chronic diseases but failing even at that.

The average age of death of COVID patients is similar to, or, in the case of Switzerland, higher than, the country's pre-COVID life expectancy, although as the

---

[98] [178]

most vulnerable pass away, it is expected that this number will decline, as will the life expectancy figure itself. [99]

The identification of infected people remains, therefore, the highest priority in effective treatment, followed by their isolation, while encouraging the rest of the population to get plenty of fresh air. In Marseilles, a city famous for its seaside restaurant and outdoor eating, closing the restaurants and forcing people to stay in their homes merely increased infectious contacts.

Government Intervention

There is little correlation between government action and the outcome of COVID-19. However, there is strong correlation between government action and a decline in economic activity and tax revenues, and a subsequent increase in national debt, with increases in taxation still a subject for debate, but no longer (in November 2020) in question.

The only prepared, sensible and economically effective response to a pandemic threat is to inspect all incoming passengers for infection, using rapid mass testing by thermometers or thermographic cameras to triage a large proportion of those likely to be infected, and then to carry out more invasive and accurate tests on those that are detected. Isolation of those infected, treatment, and tracing of contacts follows.

---

[99] Average age of death for COVID patients is France is 84 years, while life expectancy is 82.5. Research by IRMES, CNRS and AP-HP of 160 countries. [138]

This protocol, long-time and still promoted by the World health Organisation, is the most effective and has the least impact on the economy or on personal freedom. It has largely been ignored by western democracies.

Asian countries have long lived with the threat of pandemic, and have prepared, practiced and implemented the protocol in the past, to deal with SARS for example. Improvements through practice mean that island nations, such as Taiwan, which are easier to control, have survived the COVID panic with relatively few controls and very few infections and deaths.

Asia is the origin of many infections, not due to some plot or conspiracy but simply due to the concentration of the world's population and the density of its cities. The popularity of bush meat in Africa, South America and Asia, with perhaps fewer controls on its handling, may have an additional effect. However, European abattoirs have been super spreaders of COVID, and British abattoirs carry the shameful responsibility for mad cow disease, so it is better to say that there is always a risk of disease in dealing with any living organism. Diseases are caused by parasites, from viruses to large worms, via bacteria and fungi, and humans carry just billions, evacuating them through bodily fluids and infecting our family, neighbours, loved ones and complete strangers, as well as pets, livestock and wild animals. There are no innocents in life.

In the final analysis, government measures may turn out to be justified, just what the doctor ordered, saving lives. However, then governments would still have to justify their actions against the economic cost, the social destruction, the loss of years, the imprisonment of the vulnerable, the restrictions on everybody else, the cost in education and socialisation of children, and the deaths caused directly by the measures taken.

Governments would also have to explain why they did not use such measures before for other respiratory diseases, other acute infectious diseases or the chronic diseases that kill the vast majority. They would even have to justify their failure to introduce social restrictions to prevent deaths from sports, playground accidents, travel, war, and sex.

Finally, if governments are so obsessed about life, and preserving it "whatever the cost", they would have to explain why they permit euthanasia, abortions and even contraception.

Successful Interventions

New Zealand rapidly closed its borders, and has had both few infections and few deaths. However, it is now permanently locked down, with a population that has no natural immunity, and no plan that will allow it to open without suffering the consequences. Vaccines may help, but realistically they will not help more than the flu vaccine, which provides no better than a 30% improvement. Eventually, the population will have to suffer at least 60% of what was suffered by other countries, after probably years of isolation.

Australia is in an identical situation, although unlike New Zealand it has implemented some of the most draconian local lockdowns, including that of Melbourne. Most Australian COVID deaths were caused by government policy in stuffing infected and vulnerable people together, without testing, without care and under the guard of untrained individuals in insalubrious conditions.

Both New Zealand and Taiwan are relatively small island states, relatively isolated by nature and politics, and also of relatively small populations. However, other countries in similar situations have failed miserably. Britain has almost three times the population of Taiwan, but Ireland is about the same as New Zealand. Both the British Isles left their borders open, and when they closed them except for essential traffic, they still failed to implement any meaningful controls. Instead, and against all the scientific advice and evidence, they implemented lockdowns and restrictions. Ireland has suffered four thousand deaths, New Zealand 26. United Kingdom has suffered 126 thousand deaths, Taiwan 10. [100]

Meanwhile, France, Spain, Italy, all countries that did not control entry, merely closed borders to non-essential traffic and locked down the population, suffered some of the highest death rates in the world. Even before the second wave, they also implemented obligations for the entire population to wear masks.

WHO

The World Health Organisation (WHO) rightly restricts itself to medical and health issues. It refuses to

---

[100] Numbers as of 25 March 2021.

comment officially on political matters. However, that does not prevent WHO officials from making such comments in the media, even while officially representing the WHO. As media pundits, WHO officials should be no more listened to than pop stars or actors. Not because they don't have access to critical information, but because the process of interrogation or interview is not conducive to rational thinking. The hysteria of competitive debate leads not to the best or most truthful result, but to the one that most successfully latches on to the audience's emotional needs.

Published documents from WHO, on the other hand, are prepared and reviewed by scientific teams, usually in the peace and calm following major learning opportunities.

Most countries, including the UK, France and the USA, have health procedures for handling infectious and notifiable diseases. Much of this either comes from WHO or, considering that these countries have led scientific medicine for the last two hundred years, is supplied to WHO.

Major problem in many countries was a ban on using primary care, doctors and nurses in local surgeries and clinics. Instead, patients with symptoms and signs were sent straight to hospital, regardless of their condition. While most upper respiratory tract infections are treated symptomatically, at home, COVID resulted in many patients sent to hospital, where they merely overloaded , or care homes.

Examples of incompetence

In a paper published in 1991 in the New England Journal of Medicine, researchers assessed the stress levels of 394 individuals and then gave them nasal drops containing either one of five types of respiratory viruses or a saline solution. The more stress the people were under, the more likely they were to fall ill if the drops they had been given contained a virus.

https://www.scientificamerican.com/article/a-wave-of-resurgent-epidemics-has-hit-the-u-s/

The quote opening this appendix has been ignored by governments rushing to implement any kind of policy they think will help keep them in their jobs. They also need to justify those actions. Selecting options is more about choosing allies and minimising the effect of political attacks. Whatever concern exists for the rest of the population, it takes second place to the politicians own priorities.

Research also shows that populations who feel that they are at risk from uncontrollable threats, are also those that take the greatest risks, smoking, eating and behaving as if the world might end tomorrow. [101] Governments that increase the uncontrollable risk scenarios are guilty of exacerbating the problem of COVID, even before they have taken any action.

In order to justify the actions they were taking, particularly to get involved in the first place, governments around the world selected forecasts which supported their natural instincts. There is never any shortage of points of view, and those with a scientific

---

[101] [181]

label are more impressive. Governments looking to impose needed to look no further than the modelling of Neil Ferguson, doyen of COVID death forecasters and lockdown lover. Ferguson had wrongly forecast the foot and mouth outbreak in 2001, and government intervention based on it had wiped out cattle in Britain, destroying its beef export business for twenty years at enormous cost. He had wrongly forecast the 2005 bird flu outbreak, the 2002 Mad Cow disease, and the 2009 swine flu. Yet, his prognostications satisfied government need for a scientific paper that permitted them to impose restrictions, executions, and destructions.

As well as ignoring the opportunities for improving quality of life, employment, the economy, the health service, governments have ignored the opportunity to slim down their bloated organisations. Both France and Italy have recently discussed reducing the number of their politicians, but have struggled to get cross party support for career suicide. COVID presented a great opportunity, to reduce both politicians and civil servants, as well as all the agencies, consultants and hangers-on.

COVID lockdowns forced everyone to look at their role and judge it essential or non-essential. It is easy to argue that any government job that is not essential is a sinecure. Borrowing money to fund it makes no sense. During COVID, many of these jobs are not carried out, not just because they are not essential, but because their customers are not allowed to visit. This includes all the arts, culture and museum staff, which are obvious, but also all the frontier control staff, desperate for more border controls to keep their jobs, but unnecessary given the conditions in which the only people travelling are using exemptions.

Local councils have all but shut down, services to the aged, ill, or undereducated are provided remotely, many traditional services, like road sweeping, gardening, have disappeared.

In spite of the destruction of local services, no government, local or national, has suggested reducing taxes in return. On the contrary, as a sign of *solidarity*, tax-payers are expected to pay more in taxes, not only to maintain these people in their jobs, but to pay for all the others who jobs governments have destroyed, the independent artists, and all those working in the tourist industry and hospitality.

French government incompetence

One of the major interveners in France during the COVID period has been the health minister. These are a selection of his quotes along with some pertinent ones from his colleagues, including the president, translated by the author from the original French.

- 18 February, 2020. "France is ready [for coronavirus]" – interFrance interview.
- 23 February. "Every county in France will be fully-equipped and ready to face the coronavirus pandemic" - France 2 interview.
- 28 February. "Masks are useless" – at a presidential conference.
- 3 March. "Everything is ready" – BFM TV-RMC.
- 4 March. Surgical masks will not be supplied to the general public, except under prescription, but there is no shortage – a government spokeswoman during an interFrance interview

- 6 March. "Masks are not recommended, and are useless, for those not infected".
- 10 March. "FFP2 masks are being released immediately to hospitals" – Europe 1 interview,
- 16 March. No masks have arrive at the hospitals. The situation is so serious that the president is brought in, promising that the 25 worst affected departments will receive them on the 17th in the evening, and the rest on the 18th. On the 18th, hospitals still had no protective clothing.
- 17 March. "Masks are useless for those who are not ill" – the same government spokeswoman, speaking at a cabinet meeting.
- 18 March. The director-general of Health, he senior French civil servant in the Health ministry, reiterated the uselessness of surgical masks for non-surgical needs.
- 20 March. "We were a country that, unfortunately, was not ready, the hospitals had not enough masks & PPE" – BFM TV coverage of a parliamentary session.
- 20 March – the same day. "I will release millions of masks" which, presumably, he had been keeping back – in BFM TV's programme *Bourdin Direct*.
- 21 March. "Only 11 Million surgical masks remain, and no FFP2 masks in the national stockpile."
- 31 March. The president is brought out again to stem the panic, stating that "masks are ready when needed".
- 3 April. "The general population can wear home-made or mass market non-surgical masks if they want" – a new government spokesman.
- 7 April. "Surgical masks will not be made available for the general public".
- 13 April. The president announces that he supports "mass market non-surgical masks for the general public".
- 28 April. The prime minister announces that "all passengers on public transport must wear masks".
- 15 June. "I am not one of those who goes around talking about things he knows nothing about" – LCI interview.
- 14 July. The president announces that "all people in public enclosed spaces must wear masks".

- 15 July. "I recommend [wearing a mask]" – public interview, recorded and broadcast by BFM TV-RMC, while visiting a mask factory.
- 24 September. Based on the experience already seen, "the mask doesn't work so well" in preventing infections – BFM TV coverage of parliamentary session.
- "There won't be a second wave" and "[even if there is a second wave] we won't have a second lockdown".

In addition to the mask controversy, the health minister also commented at various times on testing and lockdowns, stating that mass testing is useless, and that confinement provokes the virus. Later, he was forced to change opinion, and no doubt he will change opinion again. On 25 March, he banned the use of hydroxychloroquine, except in intensive care for seriously ill patients. This went against the evidence from IHU Marseilles that prophylactic treatment on hospitalised cases (but not yet in intensive care) with antivirals and antibiotics helped prevent worsening of the case.

Whether or not hydroxychloroquine is effective, in intensive care or as a prophylactic, is something best left to the experts. However, academic, placebo-controlled studies are unlikely to end the argument. The placebo effect is well documented, in academic, placebo-controlled studies. Its effect is just as important on the patient as on the medical staff and the doctors treating them. Patients drowning in their own mucus can suffer more from panic than the actual disease, and hydroxychloroquine, with its chemical name powerfully suggestive of something that can kill viruses, administered by a caring and confident doctor, will do more than a ministerial *pronunciamento* declaring it useless.

Doctors have the obligation to treat patients as they think best, and can neither operate nor withhold treatment at the behest of the government. For a politician in Paris to dictate a course of treatment on a patient he has never seen is as ludicrous as a doctor in Marseilles refusing to give a pill that will make the patient feel better.

The doctor in charge at IHU Marseilles who led a one-man campaign against government intervention in the treatment of patients is now being charged with charlatanism and is being prosecuted by some of the pharmaceutical companies he insulted.

This example is not unique, although the extreme conditions, short time, the persistence of the politician, and popularity of the subject matter simply make it easy to detect the lies. There is no law against misleading the public, although lying to parliament is usually a serious offence.

As for COVID, the result depends to a great extent on the virus itself. Previous coronaviruses have disappeared from view, either through attenuation, or media fatigue, never from effective government intervention. Most likely, COVID-19 will just disappear to become yet another virus responsible for seasonal, or maybe not so seasonal, upper respiratory tract infections. [102]

---

[102] Previous infections, like cholera, have had remarkable effects on society. Cholera, like COVID, caused panic, although the numbers involved outside India were quite low, compared to normal death rates. However, their concentration in urban areas rendered those most voluble, the politicians, mass media and the masses themselves, vulnerable. The detection of the vector led to wholesale sewage works, starting with the cities most effected,

Viruses

The errors implemented by governments, organisations and families stem from a total misunderstanding of what a virus is, and how it interacts with humans and other animals.

Viruses are just one micro-organism type, along with bacteria, fungi and archaea, which inhabit the planet. They also inhabit the human body, and every human body, with the exception of some babies born by caesarean section, is covered and filled with them. Humans have viruses, fungi, bacteria and archaea in the mouth, throat and lungs, in the stomach, digestive system, and in the sexual organs. There are more micro-organism cells in the body than pure human cells. Bacteria alone outnumber human cells.

Humans, 15% of them, carry the virus responsible for strep throat, 50% carry the herpes virus, a small number carry syphilis or gonorrhoea. E. coli, an essential bacterium, lives in the gut of all humans. They perform important functions, cleaning the body, preventing other micro-organisms from becoming pathogenic (harmful), and digesting food. Some are true parasites, consuming resources and replicating

---

London and Calcutta, and Paris soon followed. Although waste water systems date back to pre-Roman times, and seem obvious, European governments had ignored them until

themselves at their hosts expense, even going as far as modifying their behaviour to improve their survival.

Throughout evolution, viruses entering their target's cells have added their RNA or DNA, and human DNA includes up to 50% DNA of virus origin.

Viruses are not, therefore, malign, but part of a complex biome. Humans are not unitary creatures, created in a single flash of inspiration. They have evolved over millions of years, incorporating DNA and micro-organisms to produce a functional machine that is made up of trillions of individual cells, all working in such a way as to ensure their reproduction. A virus is just part of that rich cellular biodiversity.

The greatest concentrations of this bacterial flora are in the lower intestinal tract, the colon, and in the upper respiratory tract, the mouth and throat. These bacteria, which are usually harmless in a healthy body, actively dissuade pathogenic invaders such as other bacteria and viruses from infecting the body. For example, while an attack on a healthy normal individual by Salmonella requires a million cells to produce an infection, that on a body without its floral protection only needs ten.

In order to maintain this protection, a healthy lifestyle is essential, involving psychological health as well as physical. Good food, exercise, fresh air, fresh water, and regularity of ingestion is essential. Any major changes to the body's routine can upset the flora and leave the body vulnerable.

The normal flora of the upper respiratory tract includes many harmless bacteria, (all viruses and visible parasites are generally defined as harmful, as they provide no benefits, unlike bacteria), but also some that, given the opportunity, flare up, like the streptococci that cause Strep throat. Whether they are viruses or bacteria, they live in harmony with their host, and only break out into a murderous attack. Frequently, it is not the action of the parasite that causes death but the action of a poor immune system, overreacting to the pathogen. This is a major factor in deaths involving COVID. The body decides to destroy what it sees as an invader, "whatever the cost". The cytokine storm released stimulates inflammation, produces excess mucus, floods the lungs and the patient drowns.

The last thing that the virus wants is to kill the body it infects, or the economy. A virus wants a healthy body with healthy cells that will reproduce the virions for a week and a day and infect other cells in the same body until the jealous antibodies make it too difficult to continue. The immune system will force many of the virions produced out, and these will pass on to the next host, for which the virus needs plenty of nearby recipients.

Viruses don't mind a lockdown, as it makes it easy to travel from one host to another in the enclosed and warm conditions of a house, but the total number of hosts without recent immunity is reduced. The temporary respite for the human community is only temporary. At some point, the human must leave the shelter of his home and venture out. If he or she is a politician, policeman, doctor or nurse, truck driver or essential shop assistant, then he or she will not have a lockdown at all. Probably half the population still has to travel at some point. The virus may reduce its rate of infection and mutation, but such measures will not lead to its extinction. No virus or other infectious agent has become extinct as a result of passive protective measures, and few have disappeared from the more aggressive interventions such as vaccines.

Viruses by their nature mutate. Genetic mutation is common to all lifeforms based on RNA and DNA. At each stage of reproduction, the genetic coding can mutate, and over generations the mutation maintains a steady rate. When a virus infects more people due to the density of population, it can mutate faster, when the population is less dense, it will mutate more slowly. The only thing that slows the mutation down, that also slows down the infection rate, is the immunity of the population due to a previous infection by the virus or a vaccine based on a similar virus or earlier strain. Therefore, any attempt to slow down the virus by reducing the number of infections merely delays the ultimate infection of the entire population, the achievement of the endemic state. In this state, the majority of the population have achieved some immunity through previous infections or inoculations, and the rest, new born or somehow innocent, are infected during epidemics.

Individuals who are vaccinated or have immunity from previous infections are still potential targets for a virus. The virus in the form of individual virions will attach to cells, penetrate them and start to produce new virions. Only at this stage will the macrophages and antigens attack the virions and kill them. The virus RNA is present in the area of the infection. Any RNA test such as the PCR test will detect the presence of the virus. Virions produced by a vaccinated or previously-infected person can still infect others. However, instead of taking a week or ten days to kill off all the infected cells in the body, a healthy person vaccinated or with previous infections can prevent the new infection from spreading within the body, can limit the effect in the immediate area, and terminate the infection within a day or two.

The virus, however, is not finished. No bacterial or viral infection is ever really cured. The pathogens remain, dormant, waiting for a moment of vulnerability to attack again. Given time, the immunity provided by infection or vaccine wears off. Cells that are difficult to penetrate when healthy become fragile or permeable in conditions of nutritional stress. The body's immune system is just one physiological process that needs health and nutrition to function correctly. Without the right conditions, the body is vulnerable to re-infection.

The body stores billions of infectious agents. Some hide in the complex of organs in the throat. Others live freely in the intestines. Still others travel around the body along the lymphatic system, the veins and arteries or along the nervous system. Most are maintained in equilibrium, providing essential services to the body while consuming the minimum of resources.

Most infections of the upper respiratory tract pass unnoticed, or perhaps with a slight sore throat. A salt-water gargle, hot lemon juice, rum grog or other old medicine may cure it, but it probably had little chance of developing into a full-blown feverish infection. A regular infection of rhinovirus, coronavirus or flu virus does much to maintain the body's immune protection. What doesn't kill, makes one stronger, usually.

Government measures, on the other hand, even when they don't kill, weaken the organism, leaving it vulnerable to other diseases as well as coronavirus.

Strains

By the time that this book is published, bought and read, COVID-19 will no longer be a pandemic, but endemic. Multiple strains of the virus will circulate. [103]

A virus is unlike a cinematic villain. Virions are designed to mutate rapidly. If the basic vector that was successful last time does not work, then it will adopt another. It may need no mutation at all, it is ready to go. A virus that transmits easily through aerosol may suffer from barriers like masks and from social distancing, like lockdowns, but it rapidly adapt to these conditions, and become a sticky, resistant plague picked up by the next user of a door handle.

As with all viruses, those strains which infect easily but cause little damage will survive best in the wild. Even these mild viruses can, through co-morbidity, cause the death of some vulnerable patients

Health policies should encourage these benevolent strains, by allowing those so infected to travel, meet and greet, while isolating those infected with strains that cause serious illness. The difference can only be determined by signs and symptoms.

Government Goals

Politicians hate clarity. Where clear objectives are defined, the failure to achieve them can be assigned

---

[103] This was written, prophetically, in May 2020. By March 2021, the number of named variants was over half a dozen, and there are many more that have so far failed to pick up a name with the public or media.

to the politician. Where objectives are open to interpretation, a politician can always claim that he is successful.

COVID starts with a major problem, the definition of the objective. The politicians' objective is merely to survive and perhaps to climb the political ladder. Their stated objectives in dealing with the virus need at once to frighten the population, to justify invasive and costly measures, and to prevent any calculation of failure.

This sets up impossible situations. The major problem is that governments are not competent to manage the major objectives they claim to target.

Infection Rates

What does a COVID infection mean ? Does it mean having dead or dying virions ? Does it mean having a stable population of virions, rather like the equilibrium achieved by most human parasites, staphylococcus, streptococcus, rhinoviruses which live on the skin, in the mouth and nose, the sinuses, the urinary tract, the intestines ? Does it mean propagating large numbers of produced virions through immune system responses like sneezing, coughing or excess mucus production ?

Politicians are not knowledgeable enough to recognise that this is not a simple matter. Clinical disease identification serves to narrow the choice of treatments, not to produce political propaganda. While a doctor looking at an ill patient may decide that the cause is a coronavirus, or even COVID-19, the same tests are useless when extrapolated to the mass population, the majority of whom present no symptoms at all.

A pedestrian can pick up the coronavirus virions in the street, and pass them from hands to mouth or eyes. Later on, a swab can remove them, and a test can prove positive. There is no evidence that the virions have penetrated any cell wall, are reproducing successfully, and have so far avoided the immune systems defences.

The virions can be dead, incapable of successfully penetrating a cell and reproducing. Even so, in all these cases, a political process can identify an individual as infected.

In these cases, there is at least a positive identification for coronavirus. However, during 2020, doctors were certifying the presence of coronavirus based on symptoms alone, a notoriously imprecise practice, given the proliferation of other upper respiratory tract infections, and the fact that most symptoms are caused by the immune system, which reacts similarly to all such infections.

French doctors are paid €25 for a normal consultation, while they are now paid €55 if it involves a COVID patient. They also receive bonus payments, €2 for each contact with a COVID patient that can be reported, and €4 if it includes their social security number.

This is just one way in which the death count for COVID has been inflated by government interventions. Perhaps these were well meant, but without a reasonable control, they led directly to the panic-inducing numbers of deaths, which permitted the spiral of more government intervention.

Other interventions that have increased the numbers of infected include the obligatory testing for contacts, for certain key workers like those in hospitals or care homes, for travellers, for anyone with any kind of respiratory infection symptoms. None of these measures have been used before in Europe to track other respiratory infections, and they immediately inflated the importance of COVID in comparison to the regular flu, colds or chronic illnesses.

The number of tests balloons as any positive test is automatically followed by more tests. A single person can test positive multiple times for the same infection.

Not only does the inflated infection figure affect government interventions, but it also affects the death count.

The Death Count

Once identified as a positive COVID carrier, any person who subsequently dies is listed as a COVID death. A few brave doctors ignored instructions from their bosses, which stipulated that they do so in all such cases, and merely put the most important morbidity as the cause of death.

Car accident victims, cancer deaths and sportsmen are all added to the list of COVID deaths, as long as their deaths occurred within 28 days of a positive test.

In spite of the poor quality of statistical control, the death rate of COVID is high, and the disease is both a challenge to the medical profession and to those patients who suffer from it. However, the conscious corruption of data to make a political point is one of the main reasons for public suspicion about any of the pronouncements and measures implemented.

Different countries at different times count deaths in different ways. For example, in Spain, the numbers for flu come from only 16 regions out of 20, from 555 general practitioners and 217 paediatricians, working with 20 laboratories. The numbers they produce are useful only for comparison with previous years, not as a guide to the prevalence of flu in Spain, or for comparison with other illnesses in Spain or for flu in other countries.

In Spain in 2017, 48,000 people died from all causes handled by pulmonary specialists, a number that included only a small number of flu patients. The numbers for flu deaths in Spain in 2017 is variously related as 15,000 by the Instituto de Salud Carlos III, and 1,175 by Statista web-site. This wide variety of numbers should warn anyone looking at COVID statistics. About 47,000 deaths in 2020 were allocated to COVID, a similar number to 2017 without COVID. Even these numbers, from the health ministry, were considered low by the Spanish statistics office (INE), who added another 18,557 deaths that showed symptoms compatible with COVID. These symptoms could also have been compatible with rhinoviruses, other coronaviruses, flu viruses, and allergies.

It seems likely that the number of flu deaths (deaths in which flu has had an impact, either directly leading to pneumonia, or weakening the patient before a secondary viral or bacterial infection leads to pneumonia, or causing additional complications to a patient suffering from a chronic respiratory problem) in western Europe has declined. This is partly due to the introduction of vaccines, but also due to the much better palliative care, hospitalisation and ventilation for what has traditionally been a stay-at-home treatment.

A likely cause of the high mortality due to COVID-19 is the success of the flu vaccination programme, which has saved the lives of thousands of old people. The effect of the increasing number of old people in the population of western nations is that it is much more exposed to the more dangerous novel coronavirus, against which they have no protection.

In the most abusive use of statistics, to show the effect of COVID on hospital medical staff, the numbers of COVID deaths announced included a quarter who were retired.

Even so, there were clearly many deaths of people *with* COVID. Whatever the concerns about the statistics, and there are many, the result would not have changed by more than 50%. The number of dead affected by COVID is still staggering, when looked at in isolation.

In the USA, the Centers for Disease Control and Prevention (CDC) is the official body which monitors infectious diseases. It counts and reports the deaths caused by COVID. However, the data it produces counts Death *with* COVID, not death *from* COVID. [104]

For 2020, the number of deaths involving COVID is over a quarter of a million, similar to the number of deaths from pneumonia. Half the COVID deaths also show symptoms of pneumonia, but whether

---

[104] US data mortality codes deaths involving COVID-19 in the reports produced by CDC. [182]

the pneumonia is caused by COVID or by another viral or a bacterial or fungal agent is not determined. Influenza (flu) is insignificant, with only seven thousand deaths recorded by CDC for the year.

COVID was present in about 10% of deaths of those over 65, with its impact decreasing below that age, to only 1% for children, similar to the flu. [105] The average age of death of patients with COVID was 78, which compares to the average American life expectancy of 78.54 years.

Overall, then, in spite of the panic, the measures, and COVID itself, COVID had little effect on life in the United States. Any disruption, suffering or pain was caused by government intervention, with the support of the population.

Co-Morbidity

The effect of the COVID virus in the type of pandemic experienced in Europe depends on the climate, the age of the population, the level of obesity, and the level of activity (exercise), not on political interventions except where these affect the above. The key factors that affect the survival of an individual infected by COVID remain the triad of age, obesity and general health, in which respiratory problems – chronic obstructions, asthma, cancer, smoking – are key.

One way of determining whether death was caused by COVID-19 is to ask whether the person

---

[105] This data is provisional. The problem of co-morbidity is understood by data scientists at CDC, and they have no intention of changing their production to reflect all the causes of death listed on death certificates. [144]

would have died without it. At the same time, however, for a patient with a co-morbidity, the question should also be asked whether the death would have occurred without old age, obesity, diabetes or asthma.

Equally, there is a case for qualifying death. All deaths are tragedies for those intimately involved, but there is a difference between an expected death, of someone dying from a long terminal disease such as lung cancer, and that of someone dying from a short term illness such as a cobra bite. A coronavirus death of a young, fit, healthy athlete is something that should be counted and countered, but a coronavirus death of a dementia patient in a care home can be counted but no special measures need to be taken, certainly none that affect the global economy, personal freedoms, or that lead to mass rioting, police brutality and additional deaths.

Those with co-morbidities as common as obesity, cardiovascular insufficiency and fragile immune systems became the major sufferers, but the virus also touched those caring for them, or simply those living in the same house.

On average, however, only those with 3 or more co-morbidities, including COVID-19, died of the combination. It is possible to say that without COVID-19, there is a good chance that these patients would not have died just then, although as most of them were over the life expectancy of their country, they would most probably have died sooner rather than later. Equally, it is possible to say that without one of the other co-morbidities, or all of them, they would have survived. Therefore, it is as incorrect to say that x people died of

COVID as it would be to say that y people died of diabetes. They died of a triple co-morbidity.

At no time has any government banned sugar, cakes, pasta or potatoes, or prohibited their import, transport, sale or advertising.

Governments don't shut down the global economy nor impinge on basic freedoms of association, occupation, and movement because of the massive disaster that is dementia, or diabetes, or obesity, or compromised immunity due to illnesses, self-inflicted injuries or accidents. Governments have shut down the economy and blamed it on COVID, but they did not do the same things for the other co-morbidities, nor do they blame the deaths on them.

Protection of the healthcare system

One argument, perhaps the major one in European democracies, for constraining civil liberties during the COVID-19 panic, is that these measures are necessary to protect the healthcare system and its frontline workers, to prevent a breakdown of care services for the general public. This can best be achieved by slowing down the infection rate, and therefore the hospital intake of seriously ill patients, by reducing human contact and infections to a manageable number.

This is the greatest lie in politics. Healthcare systems reflect the diseases that the public and politicians wish to treat. If governments want to treat larger numbers of patients, they can open more hospitals. If there are insufficient beds for COVID-19 or other patients, it is only due to the lack of budget and political will.

Hospitals are generally managed, like hotels, to maintain a high occupancy rate. No tax-payer wants to fund an empty hospital. Some spare capacity is necessary to provide room for training, accidents, and emergencies, but that capacity can be defined. Winter seasonal flu and other variables are managed in those countries affected. Individual hospitals regularly reach saturation, and just as regularly empty when the epidemic is passed. Additional healthcare workers are recruited seasonally, and managed long-term, year after year. General wards are converted into reanimation and intensive care units using well-rehearsed routines.

Major epidemics, casually called flu epidemics but involving multiple viruses, including coronaviruses, have occurred regularly every five years, and 2020 is just the latest. In previous epidemics, hospitals have reached capacity, overflown, patients have sat on trolleys in corridors, or in ambulances, waiting for treatment, non-essential operations have been cancelled.

As well as political decisions, there is perhaps also an underlying motivation provided by pathogens and human behaviour. For example, thousands of tuberculosis hospitals and sanatoria opened around the world to care for consumptive patients. These specialised sanatoria became popular in the 19th century and early 20th century. Partly, there was a profit motive to encourage this, partly it was philanthropic. In countries such as Britain, these have all disappeared or mutated to other pathological sources.

However, in South America there are still many tuberculosis hospitals, because the disease is still endemic there. Rather than close down the economy and prohibit travel to reduce the impact on the healthcare system of the disease, the Brazilians simply build more hospital beds.

In Britain, instead of TB hospitals, we now have VD clinics. Governments could simply ban sex, prohibit international travel or at least that by homosexuals, intravenous drug-users, and Africans and African-Americans, force people to stay at home, and restrict social gatherings to 1 person. This would solve the VD crisis, protect everyone from drug-resistant gonorrhoea and HIV, and require no specialised VD clinics. However, governments prefer to fund VD clinics.

A flu-type pandemic with much higher transmissibility and fatality has been discussed professionally for many years, since the SARS and MERS pandemics in public. European governments have prepared for it, alongside professionals from WHO.

The numbers of hospital beds and equipment, trained staff and hospitals needed to deal with a pandemic in the healthcare environment (as opposed to just leaving patients in the community) are well known. Advisors, scientists, and media have regularly promulgated the anticipated deaths of a community-led strategy. There has been plenty of time to organise any additional services needed. Instead, Western governments have waged war against impoverished countries in the Third World, have squandered billions in vanity projects, and awarded themselves above-inflation pay rises, while increasing the number of civil servants, poor and unemployed beholden to them through wages, social security and dole.

Britain has a strategy to provide minimal care; its hospitals are funded to the lowest level of any western country except Canada and Sweden, beaten by Turkey, Greece and China, and optimised to have a high occupancy under normal conditions, beaten only by Ireland. While most European countries maintain a quarter of their hospital beds free, allowing for relatively large increases in demand for pandemics, season flu, or massive accidents or warfare, Britain keeps only 15% free. For critical care, (comparisons are difficult as the definition is different by country), Britain is in a large group of European countries that keeps about 6 beds/100,000 population, whereas a large group have about 9, and another large group 12 or more, with Germany almost 40. The number of ICU beds can be changed relatively quickly by small amounts, directing resources towards these specialised areas, but beyond a certain growth, external factors, especially the availability of staff and equipment, also play a role. In a pandemic, with healthcare staff affected by the virus, and other countries under the same pressures to source ventilators, medical equipment, and staff, it is not possible to suddenly quadruple intensive care beds, or even general care beds.

These are all political choices. They make sense for politicians, because when the pandemic does arrive, those who will suffer most are the tax-payers who have to pick up the bill for panic actions which have no effect on the dead, because there is no treatment which can cure an old, obese, diabetic patient with pneumonia. All the healthcare in the world can only prolong the agony, or in the case of intubation, increase it. The chances of surviving it are relatively small, the costs extremely high, and the numbers involved relatively low compared to survivors treated in the community.

Some British scientists forecasted that the demand for critical care beds in the event of a major pandemic would reach 100 or even 250/100,000 population, but these numbers never materialised. Most people died at home.

Even so, the numbers involved become large when viewed the media magnifying glass. The death count becomes a magic number, inviolable and avoidable, instead of a tragic but inevitable statistic of a large and healthy population.

In the end, countries like China and Britain panicked, and built emergency hospitals at great expense. In Britain, 7 in England, 1 each in Scotland, Wales and Northern Ireland, and others in the Channel Islands and Gibraltar were followed by a dozen additional field hospitals in Wales. Tens of thousands of medical staff would have been required, but fortunately regardless of the media, there was no significant rush on critical care facilities and the hospitals were never used, so nobody ever found out that they were just the latest expression of pork barrel politics. The staff was never found to operate them, and if needed, the government would have been reduced to filling them with military personnel.

Recent jingoism has led to numerous restrictions on foreign workers. British hospitals employ a significant proportion of immigrants and 1st generation immigrant staff. A far better government behaviour to support the healthcare system would be to reverse its nationalism and welcome workers from abroad.

The number of hospital beds in any country with a nationalised health service is a political decision, but there is rarely a legal prohibition on building private hospitals, and nothing to prevent private enterprise from furnishing these if there is a demand. The fact that there is little demand, even with annual flu epidemics, and even under COVID, is a good indication that there is no need to protect the healthcare system, at least from anyone but the government.

Protection of the Vulnerable

In general, all government measures have targeted the reduction in deaths of the vulnerable population. However, most of this vulnerable population have only a few years left to live, and the measures have made these years a living hell, with no care, no family visits, an end to kissing and cuddling, stepping out and a general level of fear. It is difficult to see how such a person can ever return to living a normal life, and may have to expect the remaining years to be lived in isolation. This is hardly protection, rather it is incarceration.

Government Measures

The cost of government measures to control COVID are far in excess of any reasonable estimate of its dangers, and show no realistic effect in mitigating it. [106]

---

[106] For details of the actual cost of the COVID measures, against which government action and any saved lives needs to be measured, see [149] and [162].

Flattening the Curve

The best measures to prevent infection are regular hand and face washing with soap and water, and the use of single-use paper handkerchiefs for wiping nose, sneezing and coughing, with the immediate disposal in a medical waste incinerator.

Although some governments do promote good behaviour, none provide access to medical waste incinerators, none provide handkerchiefs or soap free of charge, few encourage face washing, and even these activities are swamped by the deluge of instructions to use alcogels and face masks.

Alternatives to these best measures are far less effective. The best time to wash hands is at home before leaving to ensure that no bacteria or virions are transferred out of the house. Fresh water, preferably very hot or very cold, has an immediate effect on infectious agents, diluting them and slowing down their metabolism (in the case of cold water). Soap has anti-bacterial and anti-viral properties, killing some, weakening others, but also lifts the layer of oils from the skin, taking with it any agents that are hiding there.

Alcoholic gels placed in shops will have no effect on people who have just come from home, having washed their hands, but could help to kill any germs picked up on metro escalator rails and door handles. Handles used to be made from brass, as the copper kills germs. Governments have for years advised the use of permanently-stainless steel or sterile plastic door knobs and banisters, but many hospitals are now returning to use brass as it is much better than these more modern materials at killing germs.

A better advice for shops would be to stop heating, and leave the air conditioning on maximum cold. This would harm the infectious agents and encourage shoppers to keep their gloves on. The best advice is to shop in outdoor markets, but these have been closed down at the same time as the much less healthy enclosed ones, or have been left open with the same pointless restrictions.

Testing

In general, testing for respiratory tract infections is not cost effective, and not recommended. Infections are treated based on symptoms, most of which are well understood. People without symptoms are either not infected or have a strong and experienced immune system that does not panic into over-producing mucus, coughs, sneezes, higher temperatures or other symptoms, most of which are produced by the immune system, not the virus.

COVID-19 is not a completely new virus. It is a coronavirus strain that may be different in some respects from previous ones. However, large parts (79.6%) of the virus RNA are similar, which is why scientists know it is a coronavirus.

Humans suffer from hundreds of viruses that affect the respiratory system, producing colds, flus, lower respiratory tract infections and pneumonia. An average human will suffer multiple infections in a single year, often from multiple viruses simultaneously. In an average year, deaths from colds, flu and other infections leading to complications, lower respiratory tract infections and pneumonia are usually in the tens of thousands.

Humans are not regularly tested for rhinoviruses, coronaviruses other than COVID-19, influenza and parainfluenza viruses, adenoviruses, RSV, metapneumoviruses or other enteroviruses. If the British government tested all humans, every month, for a year, the total number of infections would be in the hundreds or thousands of millions.

No test can prove that someone is contagious, and no test can prove that someone is not contagious. All that tests prove is the presence of the organic matter searched for by the test procedure.

Testing needs to be carried out for a specific purpose. That purpose cannot be a social control without very specific objectives. A suitable objective would be to identify 75% of the most contagious population. An unsuitable objective would be to identify anyone carrying any organic material from a certain coronavirus, which is what most government sponsored testing aims to achieve.

The problem with all testing is that human beings, like all animals, are basically a chariot for parasites. Humans are swamped in viral, bacterial and fungal agents. The idea that a human being is infected or is not infected is ridiculous. All humans are carrying virions, bacterial cells and spores but these are prevented from proliferating by the immune system. While the immune system is healthy, these pathogens cannot replicate, and will only infect others under exceptional circumstances. Testing for the presence of these agents will present positive results far more often than any modifiable danger they may represent.

Even so, some tests are more useful than others. Unfortunately, most tests favoured by European nations are the ones that are useless.

Antibody testing

Anyone who has had a coronavirus in the past is likely to have antibodies. These antibodies can be detected. They may exist for many years, but the experience with other small virus antibodies is that they will gradually disappear over a number of years.

However, once someone has been confirmed as having antibodies, it will be assumed that that person has had the infection, has successfully fought it off, has gained immunity and is no longer a threat to society.

This assumption is false. Someone who has had the disease is better protected, and has antibodies ready to attack a new infection, but the infection can still happen, the person can infect others, and can still be the source of a passive transmission, from hand to hand. However, even if they are infected, their production of virions will be small and shortlived.

Mass antibody testing makes sense to understand the percentage of a population that has succumbed to the disease asymptomatically, which can be compared to that which has been treated for symptoms and measured directly. A positive antibody testing should permit free travel and contact.

Antigen testing

Antigen testing is less reliable for mass testing than for clinical diagnosis of symptomatic patients, but is not particularly accurate any way. At least it provides some selection of potentially infectious, but no more than would be provided by sign and symptom observation.

Mass antigen testing makes no sense at all.

PCR Testing

A PCR test searches for a short piece of RNA. It does not test to see if a person is infected with COVID-19, for no such definition exists.

PCR is a laboratory process to replicate strings of RNA or DNA. A swab contains the patient's own DNA as well as DNA and RNA from any infectious agents. This organic material is reproduced many times until it becomes quantifiable. WHO recommends 30 replications to give a clinical diagnosis of a specific pathogen. However, countries like France carry out 50 replications, generating far more positive tests.

Mass PCR testing for COVID makes no sense at all. Respiratory diseases are highly mobile, and are found in the air, in water, on surfaces, and on almost everything touched by infected people. COVID virion RNA is detected in the wastewater of cities.

PCR tests are not designed for mass testing. Perhaps they could be so used, if a positive PCR test was followed up by clinical diagnoses. However, in no country where PCR tests are used for mass testing is any testing carried out of asymptomatic patients. Instead, they are isolated and their contacts are also tested and isolated. As a result, thousands are unnecessarily isolated and removed from work, including large numbers of essential healthcare workers.

PCR tests are used to test for leprosy, but even a positive result is not sufficient to diagnose a person. A PCR test merely establishes the presence of a viral RNA or bacterial DNA, not an infection. The virion or bacterium could be dead. Small quantities exist in water supplies, the air and on almost all surfaces. Just as police forensic specialists can detect human DNA weeks after death, so can paleozoologists detect DNA from mammoths that have been frozen for 20,000 years. There is no danger to humans from a dead mammoth or a murder victim, nor is there any danger to humans from a dead virion.

WHO does not recommend PCR testing on those without symptoms, for any disease. Indeed, it does not recommend any testing at all for asymptomatic people.

WHO recommendations are for PCR testing only where the patient displays symptoms, and the PCR is used as part of the clinical diagnosis, not as part of political controls.

The "probability that a person who has a positive result (SARS-CoV-2 detected) is truly infected with SARS-CoV-2 decreases as prevalence decreases, irrespective of the claimed" accuracy. In other words, when testing masses, most of whom (99% at any one time) are not carriers, the number of false positives is much higher than when testing patients showing symptoms. In conclusion, PCR testing should only be used on those showing symptoms, and only as part of a clinical diagnosis, along with "timing of sampling, specimen type, assay specifics, clinical observations, patient history, confirmed status of any contacts, and epidemiological information". No government wants to intervene with a complicated medical procedure, and so they ignore it in favour of a simple, one shot, useless PCR test. [107]

---

[107] From a WHO advisory notice. [183]

PCR testing protocols for frontier workers, transportation crews, healthcarers, police officers, which need to be carried out weekly or even bi-weekly make no sense economically compared to thermal tests, and no sense medically at all.

Thermal testing

The only technical testing that makes any economic or scientific sense is thermal. The identification of the vast majority of the most infectious patients is better done by signs and checked with symptoms. Coughs and sneezes, a runny nose, elevated temperature, pains and loss of olfactory senses are much better guidance than RNA PCR tests. Once identified in this way, the other tests can be used to identify the infectious agent.

This form of testing has been used for years in Asia, where previous coronavirus epidemics were controlled successfully. It was widely used during 2020 in China and Taiwan, and continues to be normal in schools, hospitals, offices and transport hubs. It follows WHO guidelines that the priority is the early identification of those infected who are likely to be or become contagious. Allied to observation of signs and investigation of symptoms, thermal testing can be carried out by anyone with minimal training, avoiding the unnecessary exposure of the limited healthcare professionals for a simple transaction. Robots are a common way of further reducing the need to expose individuals to large numbers of people.

Countries like Britain that already possess a video-based mass surveillance system refused to implement thermal testing, and suffered as a result.

Hospitalisation

Hospitalisation of patients should always be avoided. Hospitals are full of sick people, infections are the most serious, with antibiotic resistant and multi-drug resistant strains endemic. Close contact with other patients is inevitable, and direct contact with healthcare workers obligatory. The danger of co-infections is high. In addition, hospital treatment is always problematic. Ventilator use can lead to pneumonia.

A major problem caused by ignorant government instructions was the obligation for all COVID symptomatic people to attend hospital directly, rather than pass through the general practitioner or local clinic. This flooded hospitals with people who could have been treated at home, and needlessly filled beds with highly contagious patients.

Hydroxychloroquine

In France, the Dr Raoult scandal played out during the year. Raoult proposed using H with an antibiotic as he had often done before to treat respiratory infections. Most cases of serious lower respiratory tract infections, pneumonia, follow upper respiratory tract infections. They are not necessarily caused by the same agent. Infections by different agents, even by bacteria as opposed to a coronavirus, are in some ways worse, because the immune system has to start again. The long time between an initial infection with coronavirus and the death of the patient in hospital is the result of this succession of infections, each weakening the patient, facilitating further infections and reducing the body's ability to recover. The double prophylactic of anti-viral and anti=bacterial agents is designed to minimise the chances of secondary infections. Even while it has little effect on seriously ill patients who are isolated have probably already suffered from all the diseases they carry about with them, so rendering the tests carried out by Solidarity in Europe or Discovery in France useless, it has a major effect on patients at the start of their treatment, avoiding the need for them to pass the point of no return.

The government eventually banned its use, except for serious cases in intensive care. Raoult complained, saying that by the time the patients were in intensive care, it was too late to apply.

The government quoted dodgy papers in the Lancet and other medical journals, that highlighted the risks present with use of H and chloroquine, while denying any benefits.

Later investigators showed that the research was flawed and that H & C were no more dangerous than previously thought.

However, the real issue is not whether H or C have a positive effect on coronavirus patients in placebo-controlled trials, but whether they have any positive effect at all in real world trials. It has been known for some time that placebos have a real and positive effect on patients. The doctor's bedside manner makes the difference. For COVID patients, suffering from dementia, Alzheimer's disease, or just age-related memory loss, to suffer total isolation except for a daily

5-minute visit by a masked nurse, is enough to abandon all hope on life, and expire.

The real argument is between the government, whose members, struggling in a complex medical epidemic, are under pressure from their civil servants, their superiors, their subordinates, the press, the public, seek homage to assuage their crushed egos, and the technocrats, whose years of experience tell them what to do, without perhaps the ability to explain why they do it. [108]

Current medical competence cannot treat viruses. It can deal with symptoms, signs and psychosomatically treat the patient. However, the virus itself must be left to the immune system. Those who die from the coronavirus, die because their immune system overreacts, or because it is not capable of killing the virus fast enough and the patient dies from exhaustion. The symptoms can be treated with anti-pyretics, anti-inflamatomries, and analgesics; the signs can be treated with anti-histamines; while the patient can be bolstered with placebos, of which hydroxychloroquine is one.

---

[108] Experienced practitioners are unconscious competents. When the government ministers demand that they explain what they do, and why, they are unable to do so. They have passed through anterior stages, from unconscious incompetents, to conscious incompetents, to conscious competents, to reach unconscious competents. They no longer know what they know, they just do it. Supplying their patients with hydroxychloroquine is just one aspect of infectious patient care, but one which they know works. It probably works more through the placebo effect, working equally on the nursing staff, junior doctors and porters, as much as it does on senior medical staff.

Patient motivation is essential, when the patient is old, isolated, uncared for, and has no particular objective other than to see his or her grandchildren.

Herd Immunity

Herd immunity is a necessary stage to acquire as the human species, but its meaning is misunderstood by the media, politicians and the public. A population that has gained immunity is one in which those most vulnerable have succumbed to the disease, and those that survive are best able to resist its infection. Herd immunity does not prevent infection of an individual, nor does it prevent that individual from infecting others. Herd immunity does not prevent deaths; it merely reduces the number that will die.

Herd immunity is a social situation, in which a particular disease, like malaria or flu, does not catastrophically wipe out a population. Countries with endemic diseases, such as Europe in 2021 with COVID, have already achieved some level of herd immunity. The European population already had herd immunity against coronavirus, as humans have been infected by a wide variety of coronavirus strains for years. The vast majority of young, healthy individuals survived infection without symptoms. The only humans who die in large quantities from the novel coronavirus strain are those who are weakened by other diseases.

Lockdown [109]

---

[109] More detailed reading can be found at [148]

Asinine [110]

If lockdowns are so good at preventing deaths, why should we ever end them ?

The cost of the first COVID mass lockdown, a short lockdown that lasted on average about 6 weeks, was measured in the trillions of dollars. The second lockdown, entered in the autumn and which could only last a minimum of six months, would cost tens of trillions of dollars. Governments will inevitably refuse to accept individual blame for these errors, and will perhaps only grudgingly admit that their actions cost a lot of money, but that they have learnt a lot as a result. There was, however, no need to spend so much money to learn these lessons, as they are all well understood, and formed the basis of the health protocols implemented by the same governments, and recommended by the WHO.

Lockdown never worked in the past, any more than burning Jews or wearing masks.

The worst thing is that exempted people, politicians, truck drivers and hospital workers, are allowed out even if they are ill. For example the latest British frontier controls (as at 15 Feb 2021), aircrew, British and French border force staff and contractors, Channel tunnel, Eurotunnel and Eurostar staff, British and foreign civil servants and military staff and contractors, British and foreign diplomatic staff and their families, HGV drivers, people who are seriously ill

---

[110] Professor William M Briggs, Cornell Medical School, commenting on the idea of lockdown to prevent seasonal infectious diseases like coronavirus. Joint author of *The Price of Panic*, on Discernible Interviews, Political Psychology Series, Episode 8.

and need emergency medical treatment, regular workers travelling at least once a week, foreign politicians, seamen and merchant navy officers,

The rules are so complicated and pointless, that Specialist technical workers - sub-sea telecommunications infrastructure, Specialist technical workers – power infrastructure and Specialist technical workers – waste need to take a COVID test before entering the UK, but the likely far more numerous and less important Specialist technical workers - goods and services don't have to take a test.

The one group of people who are always exempted, who produce nothing, transport nothing, the politicians and their enforcers, are the politicians.

Other groups are allowed to pass with negative tests and quarantine, which includes all the false negatives from testing. [111]

With all these exemptions, relating to 48 different kinds of employment, it is no surprise that flu and coronavirus travel around the world freely.

Every veterinarian working in intensive agriculture knows that it is the enclosed living space and density of population that causes dangerous epidemics. Catalan health department study found that 70% of infections were picked up in the home. Spain's rigorous lockdown forced a nation that commonly lives on the street, on the terraces of bars and restaurants, to stay indoors in cramped flats with multiple generations. With schools closed, parents were forced to home

---

[111] All this is obvious; what is not obvious is that the government scribes responsible for writing these programmes could do so. [184]

school their children, adding to the density and danger of infection.

Some evidence exists that sexual acts prevent coronavirus deaths and infections by boosting immune system, yet in Britain lockdown targeted sexual relationships, specifically banning visits for sex. Meanwhile, up to a quarter of infections were picked up in hospital or old age people's homes, up to half of these due to faulty washing procedures, not from failure to wear a mask. [112]

The worst problem caused by lockdowns is that they disproportionately affect those most responsible for generating wealth. The most productive individuals are most restricted in their movement and activity. In Europe, where half the population now works for the government, it matters little whether these are locked down.

The lockdown prevents the entire commercial community from doing what they need to do to make an efficient market economy work. In its place, inefficient state markets will evolve. Technological improvements will take longer to find acceptance, partnerships will struggle to organise.

Masks

In theory, masks provide good protection against infectious agents like bacteria and virions. In practice, however, they fail to deliver the expected

---

[112] 100,000 American people die every year from nosocomial, healthcare, infections, so this is not surprising. Data from NHS England published in the *The Times* and [151]

protection. The main reason is that the longer the mask is worn, the more infected it becomes. Managing and handling the mask in the mass population cannot follow the prescriptions used by medical professionals, who use masks for the limited time possible, and then dispose of through sterile procedures until burnt, adding to the pollution of the atmosphere, and leading to secondary suffering and deaths, but few infections.

For years, French politicians struggled to pass a law banning the wearing of Muslim dress. The burkha ban was finally passed in 2010. [113]

French laws on 9th and 10th July granted the government the power to impose the wearing of masks, suspending the 2010 law.

The billions of masks, almost indestructible by nature, used in the war against COVID will remain like mines in peacetime, poisoning the environment for at least five hundred years. Whereas in hospitals, surgical masks are routinely burnt in quality controlled furnaces, private users of masks delight in dropping them as a taunt to authority or an insult to locals.

In Britain, some doctors proposed the obligatory use of masks, refusing to wait for evidence that they

---

[113] Article 1 of the *Loi du 11 octobre 2010* says that « Nul ne peut, dans l'espace public, porter une tenue destinée à dissimuler son visage », or Nobody is allowed to disguise their face in any public space. Police fined two thousand people for failing to observe the law. Other countries, such as Italy, Spain, Switzerland, Germany, Bosnia, Russia introduced local measures but not national laws. The European Court of Human Rights accepted the rule, but the United Nations committee considers that the law violates human rights.

might work. [114] While the ideal situation that they use to justify their intrusion in personal freedoms is that a mask will reduce by 90% the chance of infection, they cannot provide the evidence to support that. It may be true to say that a mask, when worn correctly, reduces the number of virions inspired by 90%. However, a mask worn all day will soon saturate, and many infections arrive via the eyes and nose from fingers that bypass the mask. Surgical teams practice donning and dumping masks, and practice regularly. Correct procedure is difficult to maintain, and surgeons in particular have helpers to do this. It is unlikely that the general population will adopt strict protocols.

Mask wearing makes no sense when allied to a national lockdown and social distanciation. While the public have the right to travel, socialise and work together, the wearing of masks can play a part in reducing infections.

There are four possible situations in which two people meet. In one case, both are infected, and the mask is useless; in another, neither is infected and the mask is useless. In the other two cases, one person is infected, the other is not. Only in a situation where someone is infected and someone is uninfected is there a risk of infection. Out of four possible scenarios, therefore, masks serve no purpose in half, representing mathematically about 98% of interactions. Only in the case of one or other being infected can masks serve their purpose.

---

[114] "It is time to act without waiting for randomized controlled trial evidence" [185] [136]

Wearing masks indoors where a member of the household is infected makes sense, where that person is isolated to a single room and bathroom, which are disinfected regularly. However, forcing a family to remain locked in to the same house all day long is almost a guarantee that other members of the household will get infected. The mask's effectiveness of reducing the chances by 90 or 99%

Masks have little effect on infections picked up on banisters, door handles, chairs, tables, packages, books, keyboards, telephones, remote controls and bottles, and may exacerbate the situation, causing itching, and fogged up glasses, which necessitate scratching or touching.

Medical professionals proposed a preference for clinical data over academic placebo-controlled dual-blind evidence. This is quite dangerous in any case, as the two should reflect different aspects. Evidence should guide general policy, the protocol for a specific disease with a specific treatment, but clinical work is specific to the patient and the circumstances which often, and almost always with coronavirus, include co-morbidities such as diabetes, obesity, compromised immune system or other viral or bacterial infections.

The suggestion that clinical evidence should take priority in an emergency implies that the doctor handling the case should have the freedom to decide on the appropriate treatment. This is the norm for western medicine, and has been since the time of Hippocrates.

Instead of letting those closest to the job make decisions, politicians and distant doctors impose protocols, obliging the citizens to behave, while taking on no responsibility. If the evidence eventually shows that there was no benefit or actually caused harm, there will be no repercussion on those who ill-advised the government. On the other hand, if the citizens refuse to obey, or doctors refuse to comply, then they will be punished.

Masks may well have a positive effect on reducing infections. Healthcare professionals use them. However, these professionals are trained in their use, and re-trained on a regular basis. They are controlled by other healthcare workers in their team, by a hierarchical organisation, professional membership organisations, sales people from mask suppliers, and they are directly implicated in numerous cases daily where healthcare infections take place, often with tragic consequences.

Even so, medical professionals rip off their masks as soon as possible, and leave their operating theatre, ward or hospital without one. At home, in public transport, they don't wear masks. In countries where infectious diseases like measles and tuberculosis are endemic, they don't wear masks.

In the street or home, it is unlikely that the mass of the population will wear masks correctly, all the time or effectively. As with condoms, some will wear them, others won't. It may be that eventually all will wear masks, but their effectiveness at reducing infection will reduce with time. The current pandemic may help to understand how the use of *niqab* and *burkha* became prevalent in certain societies. Perhaps they were originally designed to protect women from the unwanted attentions of men, at a time when there was little they could do about it, and greater need to step out into the street for basic necessities. Needless to say, today, the wearing of such masks is a sign of abuse

Regardless of the purported benefits of wearing masks, governments that enforce the wearing of surgical or other masks by the general public ignore the danger of pollution and disease transmission with their disposal. Surgical masks in hospitals are incinerated to destroy any possibility of infection. Masks disposed of in normal residential waste, especially when concentrated in their millions, and wrapped up in plastic disposal bags where the dark warmth and humidity will keep infectious agents alive for hours, possibly days, are a hazard to those working in the collection, recycling and ultimate disposal.

There is another ridiculous example of government incompetence, that of its plans to ban single-use plastics. This ill-thought-out measure makes no sense to anyone who lives in the real world. Whatever the problems that plastics cause, the problem lies in the disposal (or lack of recycling) of plastic, not in its use. Those responsible for disposal are the governments that tried or succeeded in passing laws against the use of single-use plastic.

In 2019, the year that COVID-19 appeared, 170 countries agreed to reduce their plastic consumption, starting with a ban on single-use plastics, mainly stirrers for chain coffee shops. The United Kingdom banned straws, stirrers and cotton buds, adding these to the cheap plastic bags that it had banned, which were replaced with expensive and much less biodegradable "lifetime" bags.

Barely had the shelves been swept of cotton buds when COVID tests demanded their longer brothers production for swab tests. Millions of tests will need millions of such cotton buds, and weekly tests will need millions every week.

Alongside the cotton buds that still litter streets, 2020 tourists are plagued with discarded surgical masks. These plastic monstrosities not only serve no purpose outdoors, carry all the germs of its wearer's buccal cavity, and

The final disposal of infectious material, including cotton buds and swabs, and polypropylene face masks, is the responsibility of governments. Most of the plastic pollution in nature, whether it is in the countryside or in the sea, is the fault of incompetent government. A failure to provide sufficient receptacles in the proper places, a failure to educate the population, a failure to manage resources, a failure to provide adequate disposal facilities, and an abnegation of responsibilities by offshoring disposal to other countries who find it more profitable to discharge at sea.

Lockdowns and masks together

The most illogical measure, introduced by every western democracy, eventually, in the case of Sweden, and partially in the case of the USA, is the combination of mask and lockdown. Individually questionable, the combination is murderous.

At no time is an individual, obliged to stay at home and permitted to leave only if wearing a mask, able to breathe clean air and clear the lungs. This is ideal for viruses infecting the respiratory tract, keeping the temperature and humidity high, and the immune response low. It vastly increases the chances that an upper respiratory tract infection becomes a lower respiratory tract infection, with its attendant increase in risk of pneumonia and death.

The one time that masks might be useful, when enclosed with an infected person, the mask is not obligatory.

Isolation

While European countries relied on lockdowns, Australia and New Zealand implemented draconian isolation policies that resulted in a short term favourable situation. Their island nature and distance from other continents favoured the complete isolation of the entire population, and both countries took advantage of this, as did other island nations such as Taiwan, but not Great Britain or Ireland.

Australia has suffered brutal lockdowns, yet most of the infections and deaths were caused by the obligatory incarceration of infected cases, mostly elderly, who were left without care and attention in the hands of untrained guards. [115]

With almost no cases, and few fatalities, the media have praised New Zealand's management of the crisis. Long term, however, it is unlikely that such a measure will benefit the local population. Isolation cannot create any herd immunity.

New Zealand's only exit from its isolation is a permanent vaccine programme covering at least all

---

[115] Of the 909 dead so far (January 2020), 768 died in Victoria's COVID *hotels*; of the 28,582 infected, 18,418 came from these hotels, with the infection spread from the hotels by the security guards and staff.

vulnerable people and their regular contacts, public health workers, retail and transport workers and users, lovers, children, etc. Even then, the arrival of a new virus, perhaps created in New Zealand, would have devastating consequences.

It should be understood that there is no absolute isolation in the antipodes. Ships carrying goods, aircraft carrying businessmen, politicians and diplomats, and a variety of wild animals carrying germs regularly travel between Australia and New Zealand and other countries infested with coronavirus. It is only tourists and families that cannot travel.

Isolation has never been a successful strategy for a species. While in some cases, isolated animals can thrive, even create their own species or at least sub-species, at some point in the future it will likely come into contact with the rest of the world. At that point, its population will crash. Jared Diamond compared the relative germ wealth of Eurasia-Africa with that of America. The massive population difference between the two areas was partly caused by geographic differences, but these were dwarfed by the importance of the transmission of germs, culture, trade and DNA. In the long term, germs are merely part of the package that makes up human civilisation, and any attempt to exclude them merely restricts the rest. New Zealand's sterile box experiment will end as a sterile coffin. [116]

---

[116] A good warning of what can happen as a result of well-meaning attempts at isolation is provided by the Spanish flu, which had a catastrophic impact on our species' population, far greater than that of the war that had just finished. After five years of isolation caused by the war, including separation, entrenchment and incarceration, along with the physical and mental wounds,

Vaccines

Vaccination does not create absolute immunity. The experience of British and Indian soldiers serving in India during the Raj, where both groups received the same smallpox vaccine, showed that the much healthier British soldiers succumbed more often to smallpox than the locals. Native Indians already carried some form of immunity, either through genetics or through prior exposure to the disease. The fact that both Indians and Britons, inoculated against smallpox, could still die from smallpox, gives a good indication of the limitations of vaccines.

The vaccines proposed for COVID are not particularly effective. mRNA vaccines are a modern invention without a long history of clinical audits. An inactive vaccine, one in which the pathogen is killed, provides little stress to the immune system; it will provide some amount of immunity and a faster reaction in the case of infection, but its effects will last only a few years. Repeated vaccinations will be necessary. There is no evidence that overall they lead to improved outcomes for their patients. Similar technologies are considered to reduce the abilities of the immune system, leading to an overall decline in health. [117]

---

especially those related to the respiratory system caused by poison gas, cordite, mining, the huge increase in the industrial production of arms and munitions, involving lead and other heavy metals, the sudden release from isolation led to the spread of a flu that killed sixty million people.

[117] The major reason that there is no evidence for overall health benefits of vaccines is that this is not measured or studied. [186]

Attenuated or live vaccines produce much stronger immunity, often lifetime. There is also some evidence that they support overall higher levels health than could be calculated from the direct benefits of protection against a specific disease. Just as the survivor of an illness will have a stronger immune system for fighting other illnesses, a recipient of a live or attenuated vaccine who survives will be stronger than someone who has been injected with mRNA or a dead vaccine.

For respiratory viruses such as the coronavirus, it is clear that a single vaccine will be insufficient to provide herd immunity or total protection for the individual. A double dose of the first vaccines will be necessary to provide a reasonable level of immunity. The only likely scenario is that vulnerable people will need an annual top-up vaccination against the most common recent COVID strain, in the same way that these are supplied for flu. Nowhere is the entire population vaccinated against flu, and it makes no more sense to vaccinate the entire population against COVID.

The major problem with vaccines for short duration pandemics like those for coronavirus is that by the time sufficient quantities are available for a mass campaign, the infectious agent may have succumbed to natural forces and disappeared, and will reappear for the next season in a different strain.

Flu vaccines work only because the virus' seasonality permits companies to develop vaccines in the southern Hemisphere for winter in the north, and in the northern Hemisphere for the winter season in the south. Flu is predictable enough and the vaccine effective enough that it is worthwhile, but only to protect those most vulnerable.

Flu is endemic. For coronavirus, the first step in developing a vaccine is to create endemic conditions. The travel restrictions prevent true endemicity. The conditions under which vaccines are developed are not similar to those under which COVID will proliferate once these restrictions are removed.

Even if the vaccinie is administered in large numbers, it is unlikely to change significantly the situation. Influenza virus vaccination administered to the at-risk groups is estimated to reduce the number of deaths by 37% in Spain. [118] This is a significant number and the vaccine is a valuable contribution to personal and public health but, in the COVID-19 world, a 37% reduction in mortality is unlikely to significantly change the measures used by government to impose restrictions on civil liberties.

Travel Restrictions

The most calamitous decisions made by governments in Britain, France and Spain, where the author has direct experience, come from their measures to control travel, especially to limit non-essential travel. These three countries are the capitals of the global tourist industry. The most ridiculous thing about these restrictions is that they coincided with restrictions on

---

[118] The numbers vaccinated total 55% of over 64 year olds and 40% of pregnant women. It may be possible initially to achieve higher vaccination values for COVID, but the flu vaccines have been common for many years. It will take a decade of repeated infections and vaccinations to achieve the kind of herd immunity that exists for flu.

curfews, lockdowns and masks. If curfews, lockdowns, handwashing, social distancing and wearing masks were effective in reducing the transmission of the virus, then there would be no need to close schools, offices, or to prevent non-essential travel. If essential travel is permitted, and it includes almost any journey carried out by a member of government, and it does not cause the virus to spread, then there is no reason to suppose that travel for non-essential purposes would cause problems. The lack of logic in governments' reasoning confirms that these measures were implemented solely for political reasons.

Many countries and cities already supported xenophobic policies. Barcelona threatened to close its port and city to cruise ships; Britain left the EU, partly to prevent the flood of foreigners washing up on its beaches; France had instigated aggressive border controls, ostensibly to control terrorism. Many other European countries had also set up border patrols, that between Austria and Germany on the main motorway between central Europe and Istanbul, being notorious.

Other countries whose tourist industry is affected include Italy, Greece, Portugal, US, and China. The cruise ship industry is dead, the airline industry and behind it the aircraft industry is also dead. The hospitality industry in Europe has probably lost half its trade. Las Vegas is operating at 40% of its capacity, and the visitors are paying 25% less to come.

These were major industries, but nowhere more than in Spain, where tourism represented a third of the country's foreign earnings,

Fines

In the first lockdown, during 2 months of Spring 2020, French police issued a million fines (€135) for breaches of the strict restrictions on travel, giving an idea of the scale of the problem. [119] Most of the French population was still mobile, even while theoretically locked down.

If COVID-19 really is dangerous, and people infected with COVID are leaving their houses and are capable of spreading the disease, the government would not have ordered its most valuable supporters, the agents of law and order, to interact with them in order to give them tickets. It would have been better for them to have kept well clear of them. If the people leaving their houses are not infected, then, they cannot represent a danger to society. If they are a danger, police should not go near them, much less then go on to another, possibly uninfected person that they can infect.

In all previous lockdowns, it has been the forces of law and order sent in to control the population who have been most responsible for the spread of the infection. Well fed, well housed, and in good physical condition, they are usually much more protected against infectious diseases than the civilians, enclosed, bereft, perhaps already afflicted.

---

[119] For the second lockdown in late 2020, only 285,000 fines were issued, mainly as a result of less enforcement, but also because the population had mastered the use of the paper or electronic documents necessary to leave the house. They had become customary.

The Old Man's Friend

Those suffering from chronic ill health, painful terminal illnesses, boredom, loneliness, and those caring for a relative who suffers from dementia, blindness, mental and physical handicaps, used to look forward to winter and its infectious diseases.

Today, modern medicine and technology keeps many people alive who would otherwise be dead. Long past the age of reproduction or production, even past the age of helping others in reproduction or production, the very old experience a living death at the hands of foreign carers and profiteering enterprises, ignored by their families, reduced to watching television and playing bingo.

One percent of the global population fits into this category, which is expected to double or even triple in the next decades. Many of these old people live happy lives in the bosom of their family, helped by some, entertained by others, and paid for by well-prepared pension schemes. Their minds remain alert even while their body shrivels. Others, however, have neither the finance nor the family nor the friends to enjoy the purgatory beyond a peaceful retirement. [120]

---

[120] Jonathan Swift painted this nightmare picture in *Gulliver's Travels*, and defined the difference between the eternal youth, a mind and a body, that might be attractive, and the eternal life, that is a soul imprisoned in a dead body. Even then, in the 18th Century, Swift as not aware of the even worse fate that befalls those for whom senile dementia is neither a soul nor a body in working order, a zombie, needing constant care, at least during waking hours.

While governments collected on death duties and inheritance taxes, they cared little how people died. Sons and neighbours took care of the aged when life became too painful to endure.

Now, however, governments offer pensions to and collect income taxes from their private pensions. In most western countries, governments are more interested in collecting taxes from pensions. They have an inherent interest to prevent disinterested euthanasia, even when it is in the patient's best interests, or when it is demanded by the patient.

The poor old age pensioners, dribbling with dementia and incarcerated in no-care homes, suffer an endless death for the profit of millions. This is not just politicians, but all those suppliers who take part of the pensioners' pension pot.

Those who benefit from the pensions scam include the gardener, cleaning lady, district nurse, doctor, greengrocer, butcher, newsagent, post office clerk, bank manager, travel agent, helper, and the meals-on-wheels deliverer. Together with the remaining family, they are financially motivated to keep the cash cow alive while the government or insurance company pays into her bank account. It matters not whether she enjoys the life, or whether she suffers.

Culls

Culls are common measures taken by the public and by government when panicked by pandemics, but for COVID so far they have avoided such measures.

In the 14th Century, thousands of Jews were murdered because they had caused the Black Death.

Later, it was discovered that they had not caused the Black Death.

Any vulnerable group can find itself the scapegoat for an enraged and illogical population. In the 14th Century, the Jews were often moneylenders and could not bequeath their property to their children, so they were popular targets. In the 21st Century, the Danes slaughtered millions of mink in Denmark because the head of the country's infectious diseases agency thought that "instead of waiting for the evidence it is better to act quickly." [121]

Mink are perhaps a popular animal to cull. The fur trade has attracted aggression for many yearsThe sterilisation and culling of pets, feral animals, and even wild animals is normal business in Europe. Badgers are culled to prevent TB in cows, although surprisingly humans are not culled to prevent TB in badgers.

Brexit

In the recent arguments about Britain's role in Europe, which led up to the referendum in which the population was asked whether it wanted to leave or remain, clever Brexiteers would have voted to remain, while clever Remainers would have voted for Brexit. However, half the population voted for Brexit, thinking that it was worth any cost to achieve, while the other half preferred to live as part of the European Union, also whatever the cost. Both were wrong. This doesn't make a lot of sense, so it is worth investigating further.

---

[121] [135]

Partly, this is a question of fish, whether someone wants to be a big fish in a little pond, or a little fish in a big pond. The British voted, by a tiny minority, to be a relatively larger fish in an absolutely smaller pond. This is a relative gain. The votes were led by those who wanted Brexit because they thought it brought them advantages.

However, the advantages of Brexit, if there are any, will accrue to those who can best take advantage of Britain's new role in which they can play their part as buccaneering businessmen, technological inventors, artistic celebrities and champion sports stars. It is unlikely that any of these will make major contributions to the nation's tax revenues.

Those who will profit most from Brexit are the intellectual elite, the multi-cultural, multi-lingual, international crowd who already profited from the European Union, through Erasmus study opportunities, relatively free trade and travel, transferable skills and qualifications, foreign home ownership and family connections. These people mostly voted Remain.

Meanwhile, the xenophobic, monolingual, nationalistic Britons, who voted Brexit, will find that Latin-American, Asian and African partners have long memories and even more unpleasant legal systems, diets, habits and environments than their closer European alternatives. Doing business in the 18th and 19th Centuries, when Britain's Royal Navy ruled the waves and the thin red line provided a powerful, if temporary defence against aggression, was still fraught with danger, but in the 21st Century it will require far more cultural empathy than has been shown so far by Britain's Brexit buccaneers.

Brexiteers are right that there is something wrong with the EU. However, they are wrong about what, precisely, is the problem, and what is possible to do to fix it.

There are many arguments that individuals may raise, but the reality is that all these arguments were equally valid in the years before the Brexit referendum and had little impact, and will remain the same after Brexit. Any resolution will be harder, harder to achieve agreement with a foreign government, and harder in its effects on the working classes in Britain, who will have to accept longer work for less pay.

Immigration

Many also want less immigrants, illegal or otherwise. There is no evidence, however, that immigration will lessen as a result of Brexit. Migration is far more often caused by local factors in the country of emigration than the country of immigration. The only way to reduce the attractiveness of Britain is to make Britain less attractive. Racism might make a slight difference, but the population of Britain is already so mixed, with large immigrant or first and second generation populations, that any immigrant will feel at home.

The major change in Britain from before 2015 to the time of the referendum was the change in net migration. For hundreds of years, Britain had been a net emigrant country. Britain built its empire on the fastest growing population in the world, a population that discovered, conquered and settled a quarter of the world. Even when the British population stagnated in the 20th Century, and the economy tanked in imperial decline, Britons still went abroad in droves. Canada, the United States, Australia, South Africa and New Zealand were mainly peopled by Britons, while Patagonia, the Caribbean, Africa, India, saw many British immigrants.

Immigration policy is not dictated by the EU. It comes mainly from the United Nations. The treatment of refugees and asylum seekers stems from the post-war humanitarian disaster, which was mainly caused by Britain's and mainly Churchill's casual treatment of foreigners, especially Germans. As had happened after the Great War, the Allied victors boasted of their war to support self-determination, and then forced people to accept governments not of their choosing, and instigated a mass program of ethnic cleansing.

Meanwhile, thousands tried to escape from communist forces, moving east to west, especially ethnic Germans who had lived for centuries in the Balkans, Hungary, Romania, Moldavia, Ukraine, Poland and the Baltic States. Millions of stateless people led to the creation of the UN High Commission for Refugees.

The Government pitched the idea that they wanted to take back control of their borders, but during the entire COVID crisis, the one thing that they have completely failed to do is to take control of the border. An island nation, Britain should find it easier than any European country. Other islands, New Zealand and Taiwan in particular, have successfully closed off their borders to foreign agents. Both are major exporters. Britain, on the other hand, a major importer, is beholden on its foreign contacts for food especially, but also for medicine, cars, oil and steel.

Foreigners will continue to come and live in Britain. If the economy improves, thanks to Brexit, more foreigners will come; if it declines, it can only do so to the detriment of those who live.

Trade Deals

The idea that we could somehow negotiate a better trade deal with the EU, or with any other trade body or nation state, as a competing external party, than we could inside the EU as a partner and member with full authority, is plainly ridiculous. Only by main force did Britain achieve its economic objectives, first as raiding and piratical enterprises, then as business corporations, and only last as an imperial, and unprofitable, concern. The Royal Navy, not only the most powerful military organisation in the world, but the largest in terms of expenditure, was an essential element in that global conquest and domination. Britain in 2020 does not possess its equivalent, and could not hope to compete with the American armed forces, whose budget is almost the same as that of the entire British government, more than fifteen times that of Britain's defence budget.

Apologists for British economic policy say that the real value of Britain lies in its invisible earnings, services and the City of London. However, even with the invisible earnings of services, Britain is declining. Export of services is even less than produced goods.

The real money made by the City of London is inward investment, effectively foreigners buying up bits of Britain. This includes the buying of bonds, financing the British government, which is then beholden to Russian oligarchs, Arab sheikhs, and communist commissars, the very same foreigners that Brexiteers hate most in the world telling them what to do.

The EU

The arguments against the EU, that it is an additional cost, that it is bureaucratic, that it creates red tape, that the well-meant social protection it enforces reduces the competitivity of British business, is all true, although the last is only true when trading outside Europe.

The problem with blaming the EU, is that the British government and, for that matter, most other European governments, have failed to take advantage of the EU. While criticising the additional cost of the EU, European governments including the British have failed to reduce their own costs, which they could have as so much work is now done in Europe. Britain could have reduced its on parliament and civil service, avoiding the cost of international trade, diplomacy, industry, health, and even security. Instead, it has chosen to duplicate the bureaucracy, maintaining the same number of politicians even though they had less work, and then increasing them with an additional 27 in the European parliament. Civil servants have also increased in number.

The major problem has been that British conservatives have failed to promote the culture of fiscal conservativism. This is partly due to their own failures since the early days of Margaret Thatcher's regime, but also to the general failure of any political enterprise to reduce its costs. There is even less interest in Brussels to reduce its expenses or minimise its activities, when the tax-payer is a foreigner in a distant country. This failure has seen ever-increasing red tape in every aspect of life, leading to a spiral of economic competitive decline. This affects less countries like Germany and Italy, who accidentally adopt local strategies to minimise the pernicious effects of the EU. In Germany, the federal nature of government means that tax-free operation in the *Länder* does not break EU rules against state aid. In Italy, some of its most successful businesses operate tax-free or low-tax thanks to special deals in the Alto Adige, the ex-Südtirol, which negotiated its tax obligations before acceding to Italy. Equally important, the crime and poverty of the south of Italy allows factory bosses to operate there with government subsidies.

Britain could have read the rule book and implemented a tax-free system during the devolution of Scotland and Wales, and in the frequent dislocations of Northern Ireland. Instead, the governments of the day have squandered the opportunities, seeing attempts at independence as something to be resisted, and seeking to punish both the devolved government and their populations with additional costs and limited benefits.

Although British racing car bosses are experts at reading rule books to ensure dominance in Formula 1, British nature, idleness often portrayed as an innate sense of fair play, does not encourage such behaviour. Britain could copy the Italians in areas such as Northern Ireland and the rust belt of the north of England and Valleys of south Wales. While British government has seen business as its enemy, nationalising it whenever it had the cash, the German and Italian companies work hand-in-hand with the government, supporting each other when needed. The Agnelli family who run Fiat have a long history of supporting the Italian government in its national and international activities, which in turn supports it, allowing loss-making factories in the south of Italy to continue operation under an Italian flag. Meanwhile, British ministers kicked out British owners and British managers, and the dwindling car industry is all foreign owned. Britain's last independent car manufacturer was bought in 2019 by Italian investors, although these have at least registered their company in low-tax London.

The reality is, that governments in general increase taxation. The accidental benefits accruing to Bavaria and Baden-Württemberg and the Alto Adige stem from confrontational politics, not intelligent and rational decision making aimed at creating a powerful economy. Many governments promote a strong economy, but only ever do the necessary things when forced to do so. The accession of Alto Adige to Italy after the Second World War was predicated on not paying any taxes to Rome, and the Roman government was desperate enough to accept this condition. The German Länder, and Bavaria in particular, refused to join the West German nation state, unless they kept control of their affairs. As a result, Bavaria is host to the highly-profitable BMW and AUDI car companies, while neighbouring Baden-Württemberg has Mercedes-Benz (Daimler) and Porsche.

Any idea that the EU prevents successful, profitable, global business is disproved by this concentration. By 1970, Germany was the largest exporter in Europe, second only to the USA in the world. Britain saw its N° 2 position taken first by Germany then Japan; even France overtook it as an exporter. In the EU since 1973, Britain maintained its 5th position, sometimes swapping with France, until it was overtaken by China in the early Noughties. Only since the Brexit Referendum in 2016 has British exportation declined, showing no growth into 2020 in spite of a 20% decline in the £, allowing the Netherlands (population 17 million) and South Korea, Italy, Hong Kong and Mexico to overtake it, and barely ahead of Belgium, Canada and Vietnam. [122]

---

[122] [128]

Trump

In the USA elections of November 2020, half the population voting thought that Donald Trump was the greatest American president, and the other half thought that he was the worst. The people in each group had their reasons for thinking and voting the way that they did, but both groups are wrong.

Those voting for Trump were looking for pride in their country and in their place in it. During the 4 years of the mandate, they benefited from a clearly-identified enemy, both at home and abroad, at which they could vent their anger, frustration, violence and ammunition. Trump voters are likely to be deceived by his actions. The vast majority of those who voted for Trump in 2016 or 2020 would suffer from lower wages, higher prices, and a drop in relative or even absolute quality of life. The inevitable result for some of them would be retaliation by the forces of law and order, arrest, prison, injury, and death.

Critics of Trump attacked him for his divisive policies, tax benefits for the rich, his threats to Obamacare. Their alternative is to encourage solidarity, the protection of minorities, the taxation of the wealthy and increased social spending. The natural result of these policies is the accelerated decline of the American economy relative to its neighbours and competitors;

---

[123] Ascribed to Ou Tsé. Quoted by Otto Skorzeny. [187]

greater unemployment, lower wages, more imports, more immigration. America's economic power is still so superior to even its greatest competitor that no significant change is likely to appear overnight. However, no marked improvement is likely to appear, either.

The actual job definition of the president depends, as with all objectives, on the point of view and the objective. A starving poor person in a backward country may have an idealistic dream that the president will provide food, water, work and better conditions, but there is no reciprocal relationship.

A leader demands only homage, service and contribution from his followers, and offers only ephemeral promises of protection and non-intervention in mate selection.

The only people who have some power to force a president to satisfy their demands are the lenders and tax-payers who finance his activities, and the members of government who manage the collection and disbursement of taxes. Therefore, the job of the president is to satisfy those relationships.

The largest number of stakeholders, usually, is of tax-paying citizens. Whatever these people claim to want, and that is an interesting but separate subject, what they need in a relationship with the tax-collecting authorities in order to support a stable society, a growing economy and population, preferably ones that grow faster than the neighbours, is a tax system that leads to improvement, that is predictable, stable and light.

Countries need their economy and population to grow faster than that of their neighbours because otherwise these neighbours will invade and conquer them. Whatever economic conditions exist today for the majority population, these can only decline tomorrow when in a minority, or even just in a smaller majority. The most important job of a president is to maintain the majority in a majority. The only way to achieve this is to grow the economy and population faster than other countries.

In this role, Donald Trump has understood, like others before him, that immigration is a bad thing. However, he has misunderstood. Immigration is a symptom of a bad thing, not a bad thing in itself. The bad thing that needs correction is the poor economic condition of the country and the resulting poor natural population growth.

Trump's decision, presumably with the support and after advice, makes little sense. China is in GDP terms poorer than the USA, but in cashflow, manpower and ability to concentrate its resources, much superior. The US is mired in pointless wars around the world, and already struggles to maintain its forces on station in spite of large numbers of reservists and mercenaries.

Trump's decision is similar to that of France to attack Britain in the 18th Century. France was the hegemon, but much smaller Britain was highly profitable. France's wars only hastened Britain's rise to global superpower.

China's economic advantage stems from low labour cost. Its focus on electronics, like its previous skills in silk weaving, may have come from specific anatomical features, but these are only valuable when their cost is competitive. China's huge population, its government-subsidised survival, and low level of luxury expenditure provides a large force of labour at low cost.

China's culture (shared by many Asian communities) has always supported local taxation, especially within families, where one member is financed through education or foreign indentures, who will then remit to provide finance for others. This not only helps with emigration and integration, but creates a tax-free business often untouchable to the money-grabbing hands.

Finally, China's government has used its rapidly growing revenues to invest in infrastructure. Cement, concrete, motorways, airports, telecommunications. China has forced foreign investors to share technology, allowing the development of its own car and rail industry

China's greater problem is its population stagnation. While it may have little effect on the quality of life of its citizens, at least for a while, it will in the long term destroy its chances of replacing the United States as the global hegemon, if that was ever the intention of its leaders.

Attempts to remove Trump as president using impeachment and the 25th Amendment are inherently anti-democratic. Presidents are elected by public vote through electoral colleges, and not through Congress. Congress can physically remove a president or make it impossible for him to operate, but only the public through another vote can replace him, democratically. Any other situation is an oligarchical coup. Whatever the pros and cons of democracy, removing Trump is a disaster for democracy. It can only lead to such situations occurring when Congress has sufficient support to remove someone, as happens in the British system, whenever Parliament has the support to remove a prime minister, who has been elected by popular vote in a nationwide election.

Economic Growth

Trump has done two things to improve the American economy, and two things to stifle it.

The relaxation of environmental policies to permit gas and oil fracking, along with a tax stimulus for the middle-classes

However, these positive steps are undone or perhaps swamped by the trade war with America's biggest partner, China, and the immigration war with its most populous neighbour and source of many of its industrial components and supplies.

Trump was right that China represents the greatest threat to American hegemony. However, this does not mean that the right response is a trade war, nor that it is intrinsically a bad thing. The USA has a huge trade deficit with China because China produces manufactured goods at a fraction of the price that the US can produce them. There is nothing illegal, immoral or unbusinesslike about this. Americans profit from the opportunity to source their wants at better prices than they could otherwise manage.

Trump's trade war has resulted in increased or new tariffs, which in turn result in higher prices for American citizens, by definition a bad thing. American exports are also reduced, another bad thing.

Trump's mistake was to think of America as a manufacturer. The US has never been a great manufacturing exporter. Britain, Germany and Japan have always outperformed it.

Population Growth

If governments in America and abroad have handled the economy badly, they have also handled the population just as well.

The simple way to keep population growing is to have a healthy economy. A healthy economy leads to early marriage and lots of kids. Women can stay at home and look after the children. Countries with growing populations produce lots of young men and women who concentrate on developing the economy.

A weak economy by definition has a large percentage of its population in non-productive and non-reproductive activities. They concentrate on improving quality of life, health and safety, preserving the environment and the cultural heritage, all activities which stifle the economy.

Some attempts at forcing certain behaviours, such as prohibiting contraception and abortion, are self-defeating, unless supported worldwide. Avoidance and evasion are more powerful. Countries like Ireland that tried this have suffered from increased emigration as a result.

Government action to support teenage pregnancies and single or young mothers will do more good, while government and media persecution will harm the population.

War Leadership

Critics of Donald Trump denigrate him with ad hominem insults. They may be right that in a business career he has lost more than he has gained, his personal habits are grotesque and he is unable to maintain the thread of any argument. However, these are not accusations that should worry a president, much less the president of the United States.

The job of POTUS, president of the United States of America, is not, as some are led to believe by the endless propaganda of the office of the POTUS, the leadership of the free world. Nor is it to be kind to old ladies, to welcome the poor of the world, to be truthful, honest, sincere, transparent or good.

A president's job is to lead. He must not show fear in front of his nation's enemies, but must confront them, defeat them in any way he can, preferably in the most efficient way, but certainly in the most effective way. He can use subterfuge, he can lie, cheat, steal, he can send his own troops to their doom, as long as in the end he brings victory. Above all, he must be seen to be the leader, to be the focus of all the enemies' hatred for his country.

As a war leader, Trump is unsurpassed. There is no doubt that in a pub fight, Trump is the one person that people want on their side, even if he is going to be the one starting it. The only other western leaders of his stature as brawlers would be Britain's Boris Johnson and Russia's Vladimir Putin. There is nobody in the EU Europe who could physically stand up to the 290lb Kim Yong-un, or even the not-much-lighter Xi Jinping, who survived a traumatic childhood and spells in concentration camps, and still regularly batters his opponents when necessary, which is not often.

Trump never promised to close down Guantanamo Bay, but he did promise to pull out of the unwinnable wars in the Middle East. He agreed to pull US forces out of Afghanistan, a promise which his loss in the 2000 elections puts at risk. This retreat would have been only the second in American post-Saigon history, after the retreat from Kuwait in 1991 by George H. W. Bush. Retreats are often seen as a defeat, so it takes a courageous or oblivious politician to make one; the preferred political choice is just to continue, leading to the endless wars of the Middle East and South-East Asia.

As a diplomat, Trump excelled in two areas. In his decision to back Israel unconditionally and ignore the Palestinians his administration succeeded in gaining recognition for Israel by four Arab nations, the wealthy states of Bahrein and the UAE, as well as Sudan and Morocco. The first diplomatic success by any Republican president in the Middle East, his achievements dwarf those of Democrats Jimmy Carter (large but poor Egypt) and Bill Clinton (tiny and poor Jordan). [124]

---

[124] The failure by most foreign politicians to "solve" the Middle East question might be perplexing, except that they mostly tried to satisfy every stakeholder. Trump simply ignored this

Totally unpredictable, Trump could decide to follow almost any policy, and he often decided to follow them all, reversing course not once but several times in his dealings with Russia, China and North Korea.

His unpredictability perhaps helped to avoid any new wars, although some might claim that he has done much to instigate a war on his southern border, and to weaponise The Wall, or even just the concept of the wall. However, Donald Trump is the first president since Gerald Ford not to send US troops into action in a foreign country and, together with Herbert Hoover, these are the only presidents since the 19th Century. [125]

No US president has achieved so much in foreign policy since Roosevelt. Critics may not like some of his achievements, but the fact that he achieved something cannot be denied.

---

impossible task and selected the one stakeholder that could best satisfy him.

[125] This point is likely to raise a number of heckles, so here is a list of presidents with one ordered attack. Obama – bin Laden's assassination in Pakistan; Bush – Iraq; Clinton – Kosovo; Bush – Iraq; Reagan – Granada; Carter – Iran hostage rescue; Ford – 0; Nixon – Cambodia; Johnson – Vietnam; Kennedy – Cuba; Eisenhower – France; Truman – Korea; Roosevelt – Japan; Coolidge – Panama; Harding – Venezuela; Wilson – Dominican Republic; Taft – Honduras; Roosevelt – Nicaragua; McKinley – Cuba. Prior to America's attack on Spain in 1898, most American warfare targeted its own citizens, although the odd invasion of Canada, Mexico and the Barbary Coast helped to liven things up. Trump may not have ordered US troops into new engagements, but he did order missile and drone attacks in Syria and Iraq.

Citations

[11]   A. Smith, *The Wealth of Nations*. Strachan Cadell, London, 1776.

[22]   E. Waugh, *Scoop !* Chapman & Hall, London, 1938.

[23]   K. Armstrong, *The History of God*. A. Knopf, New York, 1993.

[25]   W. Trotter. *Instincts of the Herd in Peace and War*. 1916.

[56]   C. Barnett, *The Audit of War*. Macmillan, London, 1986

[128]   D. Workman, *World's Top Exports*. Available: WorldsTopExports.com. Accessed 14 November 2020.

[129]   M. M. F. Henry M. Gelfand, *A Critical Examination of the Indian Smallpox*. American Journal of Public Health, vol. 56, no. 10, pp. 1634-1651, 1966.

[132]   W. Shakespeare, First Folio - *The Tragedy of Julius Caesar*. London: Edward Blount and William and Isaac Jaggard, 1623.

[135]   R. Mellen, *Denmark Mink Cull*. Washington Post, Washington, 18 November 2020.

[136]   E. R. Shell, *Act now, wait for perfect evidence later, says 'high priestess' of U.K. COVID-19 masking campaign*. Science Magazine, Washington, 2020.

[138]   De Larochelambert Quentin, Marc Andy, Antero Juliana, Le Bourg Eric and Toussaint Jean-François. *Covid-19 Mortality: A Matter of Vulnerability Among Nations Facing Limited Margins*

of Adaptation. Frontiers in Public Health, vol. 8, p. 782, 2020.

[139] J. H. P. and S. M. Sean Zeigler. *War and the Reelection Motive: Examining the Effect of Term Limits.* Journal of Conflict Resolution, vol. 27, no. 1, pp. 1-27, 2013.

[141] *Offenses.* Federal Bureau of Prisons, 21 November 2020. https://bityl.co/6CJn. Accessed 28 November 2020.

[142] P. Nolan. *The cruel peace: killings in Northern Ireland since the Good Friday Agreement.* thedetail, 23 April 2018. https://bityl.co/6CJp. Accessed 29 November 2020.

[143] F. Rolfe. *Don Tarquinio: a kataleptic phantasmatic romance.* London: Chatto & Windus, 1969.

[144] *Provisional COVID-19 Death Counts by Sex, Age, and State.* CDC. https://bityl.co/6CJw. Accessed 7 December 2020.

[145] M. Anderson, Director, *Logan's Run.* USA: Saul David, 1976.

[146] T. M. and M. Cranston. *Australia's best paid bureaucrat rakes in $2.5m.* The Australian Financial Review, Sydney, 2019.

[148] A. Berenson. *Unreported Truths about COVID-19 and Lockdowns - Part 2: Update and Examination of Lockdowns as a Strategy.* Amazon, 2019.

[149] W. M. Briggs, J. W. Richards, Douglas Axe. *The Price of Panic - How the Tyranny of Experts Turned a Pandemic into a Catastrophe.* Washington DC, Regnery, 2019.

[150] G. Eliot. *Silas Marner.*

[151] M. Discombe. *Covid infections caught in hospital up by half in a week.* 16 January 2021. https://bityl.co/6CMp. Accessed 18 January 2021.

[152] D. Korn-Brzoza. *La Police de Vichy.* France, Program 33, 2017.

[153] J.-M. B. and L. Chabrun. *Les Policiers français sous l'occupation.* Paris, Perrin, 2001.

[154] J. Kruger. *Née d'amours interdites.* Paris, Perrin, 2006.

[158] M. Keneally. *President Trump has called himself smart six times before.* 9 January 2018. https://bityl.co/6CMg. Accessed 14 February 2021.

[159] U. Dicke. and. G. Roth. *Neuronal factors determining high intelligence.* The Royal Society Philosophical Transactions, vol. January 5, no. 371, p. 1685, 2016.

[160] G. Roth. *The long evolution of brains and minds.* Dordrecht: Springer, 2013.

[161] P. Aaby, S. Mogensen and A. Rodrigues. *Evidence of Increase in Mortality After the Introduction of Diphtheria–Tetanus–Pertussis Vaccine to Children Aged 6–35 Months in Guinea-Bissau : A Time for Reflection?* Frontiers in Public Health, vol. 6, p. 79, 2018.

[162] D. Axe, W. M. Briggs and J. W. Richards. *The Price of Panic : How the tyranny of experts turned a pandemic into a catastrophe.* Washington, DC, Regnery, 2020.

[163] F. F. Coppola. *The Godfather.* United States, Paramount Pictures, 1972.

[164] W. Herkewitz. *How Much of the Brain Can a Person Do Without?* Popular Mechanics. https://bityl.co/6CLw. 19 September 2014.

[166]   J. J. L. M. Bierens, P. Lunetta, M. Tipton and D. S. Warner. *Physiology Of Drowning: A Review.* Physiology, vol. 31, February 17, pp. 147-166, 2016.

[169] S. Potter. *The Theory and Practice of Gamesmanship or The Art of Winning Games Without Actually Cheating.* London, Penguin, 1962.

[170] E. Berne. *Games People Play.* London, Penguin, 1964.

[171]   B. J. Ruffle and R. Sosis. *Cooperation and the in-group-out-group bias: A field test on Israeli kibbutz members and city residents.* Journal of Economic Behavior & Organization, vol. 60, pp. 147-163, 2006.

[172] J. &. R. Simons. *Class and Colour in South Africa.* London, Penguin, 1969.

[173] M. Corballis. *The Origins and Evolution of Language.* https://ytube.io/3GK4. TEDx Auckland 4 August 2018. Accessed 10 March 2021.

[174] P. Rulken. *Why the majority is always wrong.* https://ytube.io/3GK5. TEDx Maastricht, 21 October 2014.

[175] The Telegraph. *Frasier & Eddie the Dog, and the 24 other best comedy duos.* 28 September 2016. https://bityl.co/5xFM. Accessed 12 March 2021.

[176] J. Swartzwelder. *Homer the Vigilante.* Gracie Films, 1994.

[177] I. Slim. *Pimp.* Canongate: London, 2009.

[178] J. F. Toussaint. *Global study of public health, illnesses, behaviour, and government interventions.*

[179] WHO.

[180] IHME. Global Burden of Death. World Economic Forum. https://bityl.co/6CLQ.

[181] G. V. &. N. D. Pepper. *Perceived extrinsic mortality risk and health behaviour: Testing a*

behavioural ecological model. Human Nature , vol. 25, no. 3, 2014.

[182] https://data.cdc.gov/nchs/.

[183] World Health Organisation. *WHO Information Notice for IVD Users 2020/05, Nucleic acid testing (NAT) technologies that use polymerase chain reaction (PCR) for detection of SARS-CoV-2.* May 2020. https://bityl.co/6CLN. Accessed 20 January 2021.

[184] The Government of the United Kingdom. *Coronavirus (COVID-19): jobs that qualify for travel exemptions.* 21 March 2021. https://bityl.co/6CKF. Accessed 27 March 2021.

[185] T. Greenhalgh et al. *Face masks for the public during the covid-19 crisis.* British Medical Journal, no. 8242, 2020.

[186] C. S. Benn. *How vaccines train the immune system in ways no one expected.* Club EvMed, 2021.

[187] O. Skorzeny. *My Commando Operations.* 1975.

[188] W. D. Larson. *New Estimates of Value of Land of the United States.* 3 April 2015. https://bityl.co/6CKA. Accessed 30 March 2021.

[189] *US Debt Clock.* https://www.usdebtclock.org. Accessed 30 March 2021.

[190] Y. N. Harari. *Sapiens: A Brief History of Humankind.* Harper, 2015.

The Author

The book derives from the author's personal observation of human behaviour during 2020 in Spain, France and the United Kingdom, as well as reported observations worldwide.

He spent the first lockdown in Spain, the second in France. His work and family take him virtually to every continent, and has permitted him to experience the most draconian lockdowns in Melbourne, Australia, the 1km lockdowns in France and Spain, as well as the chaotic ones in the United States of America and the United Kingdom. In addition, he has direct experience of those in China and Taiwan, India, Germany, Netherlands, Italy and Brazil.

Brexit will have a direct impact on his life as an expatriate Briton living in France, with family in the UK and Spain. Brexit and COVID have combined to turn what was a relatively relaxed weekly, even twice-weekly Channel crossing into a physical impossibility. The border between France and Spain is at the time of writing closed except for those who take regular PCR tests.

In 1986, the author visited the recently-completed Trump Tower in New York City. Trying to buy a Silver Dollar money clip, he was told in one of the jewellers inside the building, "We don't sell anything American".

The Author

Also, by the same author:

Tax Man: How Homo sapiens *took 10% of everything to conquer the world*

Myth of England: Debunking the Brexit Bible

The River of Gold: Tax Man's Route to Wealth

Gifts from the Gods: Good for Trade, Good for Tax

bloody *bedford: The Last English King of France*

Mau Mau: Kenya Battlefield

Man with Gun: A Wonder

10 Manuels and a Manolete: A carpark-to-peak guide to the high Pyrenees